Burned Child
Seeks the Fire

Burned Child Seeks the Fire

A Memoir

Cordelia Edvardson

Translated by Joel Agee

Beacon Press
Boston

Beacon Press
25 Beacon Street
Boston, Massachusetts 02108-2892

Beacon Press books
are published under the auspices of
the Unitarian Universalist Association of Congregations.

Original title:
Bränt barn söker sig till elden
© 1984 by Cordelia Edvardson
Translation © 1997 by Beacon Press
02 01 00 99 98   8 7 6 5 4 3 2

Text design by John Kane
Composition by Wilsted & Taylor

Library of Congress Cataloging-in-Publication Data
Edvardson, Cordelia, 1929–
    [Bränt barn söker sig till elden. English]
    Burned child seeks the fire : a memoir /
Cordelia Edvardson ; translated by Joel Agee.
        p. cm.
    ISBN 0-8070-7094-7 (cloth)
    ISBN 0-8070-7095-5 (paper)
    1. Agee, Joel. 11. Title.
PT9876.15.D86B713 1997
839.73'74–dc21   96-48570

To my mothers

Elisabeth Langgässer, Berlin
Stefi Pedersen, Stockholm
Sylvia Krown, Jerusalem

and my children

PART I

The past is at our mercy.
                        —Lars Gyllensten

I

THE GIRL HAD OF COURSE ALWAYS KNOWN THAT
something was wrong with her.

She wasn't like the others. There was a mystery
about her, a sinful, shameful, dark secret. Not her own sin and
shame, no, it was something she was born and chosen for, something that isolated her, singled her out and set her apart.

And in this she found her pride, not to say: her
arrogance. To be singled out, isolated and set apart, this also
meant that she was chosen. Chosen—for what? Surely not to
wear the golden, radiant, jeweled crown of a princess. Prin-
cesses were good, gentle, and blond with blue eyes. The girl
knew that she was the opposite of a princess; a dark, pudgy,
mean, defiant little brat that didn't live in an enchanted garden
but in a dark apartment in Berlin-Siemenstadt. Oh, this early
darkness!

Still, the girl consoled herself defiantly, she had her own kind of crown, the crown of suffering, the crown of thorns, which is given to those who have "descended into the realm of the dead." For this was her mission, her vocation, and as often happens with a true vocation, hers came early, very early. And the girl heard, saw, and obeyed. She, the one who possessed the power and the glory, had spoken to her.

When the girl was still a helpless little child with thoughtful sad brown eyes, an inheritance from her Jewish father, her mother used to find comfort and help by resting her head against the knitted jacket covering the child's breast. They had a name for this ritual: "*Strickbrüstchen*," "little knit-breast." The mother, lonely, tormented and violated by her visions, read a poem to her child, a little song about the freezing winds of the cold dark world outside, about the little bird seeking protection in the nest beneath its mother's wings, and the child resting content in her mother's arms. And the mother at the child's breast, for the guilt-less, innocent child is the mother's refuge, her salvation and her sacrificial lamb. Who nursed whom? Who sent Proserpine to gather flowers that drew their vital strength from the realm of the dead? *Proserpine* was the title of the mother's first novel; the daughter never read it, it was not necessary. The message had reached her much, much earlier.

The mother was nourished by her own myths, and through the umbilical cord, which was never cut, the girl was nourished by them also. Proserpine and the infant Jesus. The little round-cheeked wax doll in the manger as the world's lord and savior, this dizzying myth of the final victory of the weak and defenseless over the powers of evil, over betrayal, disgrace, and sin—was this the myth the mother wanted to revive and confirm through the daughter?

4

2

How she longed to be one of the others!

In Berlin-Siemenstadt already, in the apartment with the long black corridor, the girl's familiar prison. Here she waited with her mother, her grandmother, and her uncle, the mother's brother. Waiting for what? "For the one you can't escape," a fortune-teller would have answered. Waiting for him who would come and lead her to "where you do not want to go." Meanwhile she sits in the dark corridor turning the handle of a little music box. The music stops, she turns the handle more firmly, gets angry, turns it even more firmly, and suddenly hears a crack. Stiff with fear, the girl realizes that the music box is broken—that she broke it. Probably she wets her pants, she does that often. Her grandmother comes running and scolds her. Bad girl! The music box was going to be a present for another child, and now she had broken it! Did the girl know this? Was that why she broke it? But she didn't mean to, she didn't do it on purpose. Or did she?

This becomes her first conscious memory.

Every day, the grandmother and the mother engage in a tug of war over the girl, over the right way to handle and educate her. Wisely, the uncle does not get involved in this struggle between two strong-willed women. It's better that way, he has known this since he was a child. Fatherless at an early age, he learned to fit into the feminine world of his mother, his sister, and the various "house daughters," adapting to their ways without protest.

House daughters were au pair girls who had obviously been invented for the use and convenience of well-bred but not well-to-do families: for a little pocket money, they assisted the woman of the house, supposedly learning a thing or two about how to run a respectable household. Why the girl's somewhat cracked family should be considered "well-bred" was difficult to under-

stand. True, the girl's grandfather had been a town architect, but
there must have been many of those, and besides he had died a long
time ago. But before dying, the grandfather had to fulfill his most
essential purpose: restoring the lost honor (or innocence?) of the
grandmother. As a young girl from an upper-middle-class Catholic
family, the grandmother had become pregnant. According to the
family chronicle, the young father of her child wanted to marry her
but was not deemed to be socially up to par. The grandmother was
forced to bring her first-born son into the world in secret and put
him up for adoption. The town architect's eventual arrival must
have appeared to the whole family as a gift from heaven, more luck
than anyone had dared to hope for. Under the circumstances, they
were forced to discount the fact that he was a Jew, and naturally he
converted before the wedding. When the grandfather passed away
relatively early, he had not only bequeathed to the grandmother
two children, a son and a daughter, but also a place in the sheltering
confines of bourgeois respectability.

Unfortunately that joy did not last long. When the
grandmother's daughter was twenty-nine, an unmarried school
teacher, she followed her mother's footsteps by becoming pregnant,
and to top it off, from a married man with three children. In this family, none of the women seemed to have the gift of cheerful frivolity.

This time the child, a girl, was neither given away
nor done away with, though of course there would have been ways
to do that. The grandmother and the mother decided to defy the
world, the world of men, but realized that this was more easily
done in the big city of Berlin than in the Rhenish provincial town
where they had been living until then. The uncle, the family's
principal provider, was among the more valuable belongings they
took with them.

But it is not possible to escape the pillory of the
flesh (the grandmother), or the realm of the dead, to which we are
lured by Pan's beckoning flute—at least not before an Orpheus

6

(the mother) has revealed himself. While the grandmother wrestled and strove, ranting and scolding, against the sharp headwind of an insulted and violated respectability, the mother became a creator and a victim of myths. Of many myths, many images, from the god who devours his own children to the god who is nailed to a cross.

The girl lived and suffered at the intersection and focal point of these worlds. The child's soul and senses were nourished by the mother's visions, while the grandmother tended to the body, overfeeding it, swathing it in ugly dresses and scratchy woolen stockings attached to undervests with garters—and secretly washing the urine-soaked panties. When the girl was sick, her night table was flooded with the grandmother's sweets. The child had a pronounced sweet tooth, and when the mother came home in the afternoon, she would scold the grandmother, throw away all the sweets and give the daughter a flower instead, a single rose. The four-year-old mourned for her candy, but she knew it was the rose she was supposed to long for and to love—even though it pricked her. Thus the girl learned to adopt the grandmother's defiant victories over the stubborn tedium of the day—"Eat some more, dear"—and to make use as well of the mother's gift for lending shape and definition to chaos. These lessons were learned at a price, but later they would prove to be the girl's salvation.

She was a lonely and, of course, a precocious child.

The loneliness was the grandmother's doing. She did not want the girl to play with the "dirty and naughty" children of the neighborhood. To be sure, that neighborhood's social standing was just a rung higher than that of an ordinary proletarian district, but the grandmother's real motive was of course to prevent the girl's and the family's hidden defect from being discovered and exposed by contact with other children. She wanted to shield her little grandchild, her daughter, and herself from the contempt and derision she was convinced they would suffer as soon as their stigma was revealed to the gaping curiosity of strangers.

The girl never asked about her father, and neither his name nor his existence were ever mentioned in the house. If she ever thought of him, searched for him at all, it was in the world of legends, fairy tales, and myths to which he had been banished by the mother. In a letter to a friend, the mother described the night of love in which she became pregnant in mythic terms as Danaë's encounter with Zeus in the golden rain.

You don't ask to be shown a photograph of Zeus.

Even though the girl sometimes imagined a life in which she was like the others, was indeed one of them, hop-skip-and-jumping from Heaven to Hell and back again, playing a game of hide-and-seek where being found was a cause for laughter and not of horror, deep down she preferred to renounce all these things and hold out at her appointed post, a faithful sentry or steadfast tin soldier.

Not for anything in the world would she have wanted to miss even a single one of the shining moments when her mother revealed herself and entered into her life. In the mother's magic sphere, the world and the child became real and alive. The word became flesh in the fairy tales her mother told, in the poems they occasionally made together, even in the chapters from her next novel the mother read to her four- to five-year-old daughter. The child opened herself up, was flooded, filled, and intoxicated by the taste and fragrance, the color and form of those words. Later on, the girl found confirmation of this experience: that one can, literally, be nourished and sustained by the words of a poem.

3

THE GROUND WAS STILL FROZEN, AND THE AIR WAS cold as ice in the morning when the commands cut through the girl's feverish hunger-sleep. *"Los, los, raus, schneller!"* Groaning,

she rose from her bunk, cautiously placed her foot on the edge of
the bunk below hers and felt the hot pain shooting through her
frozen feet. She scratched the louse bites and flea stings under
her rags, which were never taken off, because of the cold and also
because nothing was too torn and dirty to be stolen. Then she put
on what was left of her shoes—she used them as a pillow at night—
and staggered half blind to the door of the barrack.

That is, the girl thought she was doing all these
things: she felt the pain in her feet, the bites and stings of the vermin, and she heard the commands. She saw and registered her own
movements, which were slow and protracted as if in a slow-motion
film. She felt the enormous heaviness of her limbs and knew in her
bones what it means when you say that you can't or won't move a
finger. Often enough, in reality, though, she would lie there until
some compassionate fellow inmate would chase her out of bed, out
of the barrack, to the roll call. Then, at the ice-cold instant of her
eventual awakening, she would be strangled by fear: what if she
didn't get there in time, where were her shoes, faster, faster. The girl
knew that the prisoner who had made the effort of waking her had
presumably saved her life—a life she did not greatly value at the
time, but which nevertheless, unavoidably, she continued to wear
as she did her lice-infested rags.

Then began the march to the factory, where the prisoners served the German war machine for a few weeks. They never
stayed at the same place for long. Since the Allies were approaching
from all sides—it was early in the spring of 1945—the prisoners were
transported back and forth, sometimes in freight cars, sometimes
on foot, all over Germany. The girl did not know precisely where
they were at the moment, nor did she know that liberation was so
near at hand. And if someone had told her, she would have hardly
believed it or not cared at all. She had her own dream of liberation.
The savior she was waiting for, and who she knew would be coming
to her very, very soon, may have been frightening to others, but not
to her. She longed to lie in the shelter of his arms and sleep, sleep,

SLEEP. Her mother had acquainted her with a strange love poem by Matthias Claudius, a kind of fairy tale. It was called "Death and the Maiden."

Das Mädchen
Vorüber! Ach, vorüber!
Geh, wilder Knochenmann!
Ich bin noch jung, geh, Lieber!
Und rühre mich nicht an.

Der Tod
Gib deine Hand, du schön und zart Gebild!
Bin Freund und komme nicht zu strafen.
Sei guten Muts! Ich bin nicht wild,
Sollst sanft in meinen Armen schlafen!

The Maiden
Pass by! O pass me by!
Away, wild man of bones!
I am still young, away, my dear!
And touch me not.

Death
Give me thy hand, thou beauteous and
　　delicate of limb!
I am a friend and do not come to punish.
Be of good cheer! I am not wild,
thou shalt sleep gently in my arms!

Oh yes, to be allowed to sleep, sheltered in the gentle arms of death, of the mother.

But not yet. Now they were marching to the factory, where they would have to meet their daily quota, attaching thin metal threads to light bulbs. Whoever did not meet this quota or

produced inferior work was accused of sabotage and executed on
the spot—at best you could get away with a shaven head. To the girl,
this would be the worst punishment, the ultimate degradation. She
wanted to receive her liberator with her hair intact, even if it was
full of lice. "Thou beauteous and delicate of limb."

But she was so awfully clumsy, with two left hands,
as they always said at home, and the grandmother used to complete
the girl's needlework in secret. She remembered the cross-stitch
design her last pre-school class was given as homework. The little
piece of cloth got more and more dirty under the fumbling efforts
of the girl, until the grandmother worked into it a yellow duck with
a red beak as if by magic. Here, her grandmother couldn't help her,
but her guardian angel stood by her. She knew it was he (or she?).
It didn't so much as occur to anyone that the ruined light bulbs she
handed in were supposed to represent a heroic effort to sabotage
the German victory. No one doubted the sincerity of her effort to do
her very best (a fact that was later added to the voluminous account
of her debts). Thus nothing worse happened to her than an order to
scrub the latrines. And with this she was fully content and carried
out the assignment conscientiously.

4

THERE, WHILE SCRUBBING THE LATRINES, SHE MET
Anna. Anna was one of the German civilian workers employed by
the factory, and she was from Berlin. Now she was "conscripted for
service" in the armaments industry. With her dark curls and garish
make-up, Anna reminded the girl of her family's maids, who had
always been so nice to her. She even smelled of the same coarse,
cloying lily-of-the-valley perfume. Anna was surely not a "proper
girl," and precisely for that reason and because of the wild longing
she awakened in her, she approached her. (In fact Anna had

been picked up by the police while practicing her profession in the streets of Berlin and been sentenced to this somewhat milder form of forced labor.)

Whispering, the girl spoke to Anna, in Berlin dialect, for safety's sake—and Anna replied! Wanted to know the girl's name, where she had lived in Berlin, when she had been forced to leave their common hometown. For the first time in ages the girl was noticed and called by her name. She became Cordelia again, Dela, from Berlin-Eichkamp, defined and really there. Thanks to Anna.

Someone was coming into the latrine, and the two of them hastily made a date. The next day, Anna gave the girl a piece of bread and a small piece of minutely checkered flannel, which she could use as a scarf. For a long time the girl stood in front of the latrine's spotted shard of mirror glass, arranging the soft material, for Anna had said that the dark blue shades matched the girl's eyes.

Naturally, all contacts between inmates and civilian workers were punishable by death, but Anna was not afraid; she was careful and cunning, but not fearful. "They can kiss my ass," she said, laughing. The girl's fear was all the greater, and when her transport moved on after a few days, it was almost a relief, despite her longing for Anna. For a while the girl was accompanied by the image of Anna laughing, by the scent of her perfume, and there was the soft cloth around her neck.

5

THE MORNING ROLL CALL TOOK PLACE IN THE HARD, pitiless glare of the arc lamps, but during the march to the factory, to yet another factory, yet another camp, a merciful darkness enveloped the women. The path led across silver-grey, frost-covered meadows and fields, framed and protected by a fringe of dark woodland, Adalbert Stifter's *"schöner deutscher Wald."* Like all the others, the girl mechanically kept to the marching beat, *LINKS, zwei, drei, vier, LINKS, zwei, drei, vier, links, links* . . . But inside, she swayed to the familiar rhythm of her own magic formula, this too a gift of her mother and of the poet Matthias Claudius. Within its shelter, the girl was invisible and unreachable, here she could rest.

> *Der Mond ist aufgegangen,*
> *(Links, zwei, drei, vier)*
> *Die goldnen Sternlein prangen*
> *Am Himmel hell und klar;*
> *(Links, zwei, drei, vier)*
> *Der Wald steht schwarz und schweiget,*
> *Und aus den Wiesen steiget*
> *Der weisse Nebel wunderbar.*

> The moon has risen,
> the golden stars stand bright and clear
> resplendent in the sky;
> the forest stands black without a sound,
> and from the meadows rises
> the white mist wondrously.

All this was present, right in front of the girl's eyes, the dark forest and the mysterious morning mist, it was offered as a gift. She walked and walked, forgetting her gnawing hunger and the pain of exhaustion, she walked straight into the luminous eternity of the poem and let it fill her through and through.

And she remembered other fragments from this poem which said everything else that had to be said, and that could be.

> *Wollst endlich sonder Grämen*
> *Aus dieser Welt uns nehmen*
> *Durch einen sanften Tod!*

Verschon uns, Gott! mit Strafen
Und lass uns ruhig schlafen!
Und unsern kranken Nachbarn auch!

If you would but take us at last
without agony from this world
by a gentle death!
Absolve us, God! from punishment
and let us sleep in peace!
And our sick neighbor too!

The girl especially liked the plea for the sick neighbor. She didn't know why.

When they entered a small town—the factory stood on its outskirts—it was still dark behind most of the windows, but in the bakery the daily bread of the good citizens was already being baked. What an indescribably lovely fragrance streamed out through the open door! The girl drew it deep into her lungs and into her stomach and was immediately a little less hungry.

On such mornings she felt as if her mother and her grandmother had finally made peace and joined forces and sworn to apply their strong wills to preserve and protect the girl.

6

IN WHAT WAY WAS SHE DIFFERENT, WHAT WAS WRONG with her? When the child pondered this question it was like staring into a dark, empty hole. There was nothing, absolutely nothing. And yet, perhaps a sense of lack, of something missing, but what? If the uncle had been something other than an indescribably good-natured, modest, self-effacing neuter, then perhaps he might have been the answer to the child's question—the girl might have "bor-

rowed" from him what she herself lacked. Uncle Heini's strength,
his tenacious patience, his gift for silent endurance awakened no
admiration in the girl; this wasn't what she needed, at least not
then. The grandmother, too, was no help here, she didn't count,
as it were, she smelled old, she was like paper on which no one
had written or would ever write.

But the mother, oh yes, the mother had what the girl
lacked, definitely. This lack had no name, but when the mother
showed herself in riding breeches, polo shirt, and boots or in her
tailored black outfit with the shining red blouse, then the daughter
became especially conscious of her painful imperfection and loved
her mother with the humble devotion of a page.

That the mother herself suffered from what she
considered her "ban" was something the girl was completely unaware of. Nor was she able to interpret the lines of poetry in which
the mother expressed her dream of redemption and paradise:
*"Beides ward ich: Weib und Mann / Allnatur, erlöst vom Bann, /
Wurzel und Arom."* (I became both: Woman and man / Allness
of nature, released from the ban, / Root and aroma.) The girl
ascribed the electric tensions in the atmosphere surrounding
the mother to the debilitating and healing process of creation.
"Mama is writing!" These words filled the daughter with the same
shuddering awe as that moment at Mass when the priest raised the
host and the brittle sound of little bells proclaimed that the miracle
of transformation was happening. Mama is writing—the mystery
is unfolding.

"THE CHILD NEEDS A FATHER." EVERY ONCE IN A
while, these words could be heard among the adults. What for? the
child asked herself. They could just as well have said: "The child
needs an elephant." Besides, it was said in the same sighing tone as
in: "The child needs cod-liver oil. The child needs castor oil." The
child had a sense that a father was a necessary, possibly useful, but
certainly not a pleasant thing to have.

When a man began to enter this feminine world more and more often, the child did not yet associate this with the concept "father." But the girl sensed that the mother would change when he was around, that she became overwrought and excited in a new and therefore frightening way. It also seemed that the mother was intent on creating a new and previously unknown distance between herself and the daughter. Suddenly the child was to be treated like a CHILD. That hurt and offended her.

The grandmother, too, seemed alarmed. She kept grumbling to herself and seemed to be full of evil premonitions. The uncle discreetly withdrew to the periphery, as usual. The girl's first encounter with the man unfortunately coincided with her first visit to the circus. She came home in a state of wild and happy excitement, was "dolled up" by the grandmother and led into the mother's room. Here the mother officiated in front of the cult objects of the artfully set table, the bubbling glass sphere of the coffee machine, the minuscule cocktail sandwiches and the pastel-colored, glazed little cakes. The child was led to the guest. She made a curtsy. He asked her what was the funniest part of the circus. The funniest? The child didn't know. The clowns hadn't been funny, they had almost brought her to tears, but the most beautiful part, oh! the most beautiful part was the rope dancer, oh, how wonderful she was!

All she had on was a little lace dress with spangles and NOTHING else! The girl's excitement filled the room with a strong and at that moment unwanted air of eroticism. Actually the child's delight had been aroused by the fearful pleasure of watching this dance performed in defiance of death, and by the irresistible fairy-tale shimmer of the little lace dress, which confirmed the danger and canceled it at the same time. The girl had recognized herself in this apparition: she too performed stunts on a slack rope without a safety net, although what she wore was just an undervest and a pair of slipping, scratchy wool stockings. It should have been a glittering lace dress too, the girl found.

The mother laughed nervously, a laugh that did not
bode well. The man did not seem to notice and smiled in a friendly
way. But the girl knew that she had revealed something (about
herself, about the mother?) that should have been kept hidden.

Much later the daughter realized that this man
had been chosen to save the mother from herself. This tall, blond,
blue-eyed man had been assigned the role of her Orpheus, her
Parsifal, her redeemer. Perhaps it was not even by chance that out-
wardly he corresponded to the archetype of the "Aryan," the pure,
unsullied hero of Wagner's opera. The counterpart to the two Jewish men who had enticed, seduced, and abandoned the mother;
for that was no doubt how she saw her own father and the father
of her daughter.

Did she not see what her daughter saw, what awak-
ened the girl's helpless tenderness? Did she not see that this man
still had the same defenseless brow, the same hurt eyes and the
same tormented mouth as he did in the photograph taken years ago
when he was still a novitiate at the Benedictine monastery of Maria
Laach? The good monks had seen and understood and very promptly
sent him back out into a world for which his thin-skinned nature
was even less fit than it was for the monastic life.

No, the mother did not see it. As always she imagined
and created her own reality, the world she happened to need at the
moment.

7

THE MOTHER IS RELIEVED AND HAPPY. THE DAUGH-
ter is going to be sent away for the summer vacations to good
friends of the mother's in Oberstdorf, an idyllic town in the Allgäu.
That is where the mother and the stepfather (can you have a stepfather when you never had a father?) spent their honeymoon. The

fresh air, the natural country life, and the company of the friends' children, guaranteed neurosis-free—all this should do the girl good. No, the eight-, nine-, ten-year-old girl (already the years are beginning to blur) was neither sick nor weak. She was just felt to be a general nuisance, precocious and difficult—there had to be some fundamental defect. The M.'s, both of them doctors, and their blond, blue-eyed children would no doubt have a wholesome influence on the girl.

Later, the girl would have no memories of that summer vacation—except for a single scene. But that scene was burned into her, seared into her soul as the Auschwitz number was later seared into her arm.

In the vestibule of the M.'s house. The girl had just come in with a son of the family, they have been playing outside. Uncle M. has gripped her arm, is beating her and shouting, beside himself with rage. She tries to tear herself loose, but is paralyzed by fear. His large red face under the straw-colored hair is close to her own frozen mask. "That's what happens when you bring a filthy Jewish brat into your house," he roars and pushes her away with disgust.

What was he so mad about? She no longer knows. But she does! It occurs to her—wasn't that how it was?—that the girl and the blue-eyed son had played forbidden games and been caught. Yes, that's how it was. Yes, she was a filthy Jewish brat. Yes, it was she who had seduced the blue-eyed boy, she was no longer Grandmother's chubby, badly dressed little girl, now it was the stepfather who selected her clothes, clothes that emphasized the girl's curious androgynous charm. The blue-eyed boy had found their games exciting, but now the idiot was standing there with his head hanging, ashamed, like a dog with its tail between its legs. The girl felt defiance growing inside her, a strong, beautiful defiance, she will not cry, won't ask for forgiveness, she will keep her face rigid, won't show any emotion. She can cry later, in the bathroom, that's something she often does. But she feels that her panties are wet—just don't let them see it!

A filthy Jewish brat—what is that, anyway? Does it mean wetting your pants and playing forbidden games? But she's really a pious little Catholic girl who took her first communion several years ago. She can recall the feeling of that day whenever she wants, the goodness and the innocence, the light and the purity all the way from deep inside to the white dress outside and the wreath of white tulle roses in her hair.

The girl doesn't understand. But oh, how she hates them, hates them, hates them. All of them, all of them—and most of all maybe herself. But her mother she cannot and will not hate. It's her mother who sent her, dispatched her to Oberstdorf in the Allgäu, a village that flaunted a sign at its entrance saying "Jews are not wanted here." The sign had been set up opposite the cross that had always stood there. The mother placed her with the M.'s, who are ardent Nazis and active members of their party. But no, she wouldn't dare to hate the mother; for to be that mother's daughter, her witness and emissary, means to be chosen and elect.

Many years later, the girl learns that the mother has written a short story about the anti-Jewish sign and the cross, a very good story. She also learns that the mother was not unaware that the M.'s were devoted Nazis and that they knew the girl's father was a Jew. But this knowledge never became a part of her reality. After all, the M.'s were her friends! It was unimaginable that they would do anything to harm her child! And besides, the girl was always writing such cheerful letters home, saying how pretty everything was, how much fun she was having, how nice those people were to her.

8

THE MOTHER HAD MARRIED AND THE CHILD HAD gotten a father. Now she would get to be like all the others and feel like them too. But the girl resisted; all things considered, she had payed a price, a steep price, for being the singular, chosen one, the one set apart. And darkly she sensed that no matter what, she would never be able to be like all the others. They were just different. She made her little pathetic attempts to defend her exceptional status, and especially the secret pact that existed between herself and her mother. The girl knew that there was such a pact, even though at that time the mother pretended not to know anything about it. Generally, all attempts to remind the mother only earned the girl mockery and ridicule.

Like that radiant, late summer day when she set forth on her first day of school, holding the mother's hand, with the traditional large cornucopia in her arm. The teacher asked whether any of the children knew how to read. Yes indeed, the girl could read, fluently. "So what do you read, little girl?" "I read my mother's novels!" The teacher laughed indulgently, and the mother scolded her all the way home.

The family, including the grandmother and the uncle, had moved to a house of their own with a small garden on a street called "Eichkatzweg," "Squirrel Road," in Berlin-Grunewald, and the mother spoke gleefully of the cozy little squirrel nest where they would all be very happy together. ("I wish you, not happiness, but the strength to bear your fate.") The child was to be a child among other children. With a shudder she remembers the time when she was forced to pay for the right to enter the hated world of that circle of friends.

In front of the house there was a little lawn with a fence that was barely three feet high. The children of the neighborhood are balancing on the fence and nimbly skipping up and down, swift as squirrels—or weasels. The girl stands apart and doesn't dare. Silly games for silly kids, she tells herself, I just don't feel like it. The stepfather observes the scene from the window, comes out and firmly lifts her onto the fence: "Go ahead, jump! It's not dangerous. All the others are doing it too." But she is not like all the others, she doesn't want to, she can't, she doesn't dare. Carefully and as incon-

spicuously as possible she climbs back down from the fence, but
there is no mercy, she is lifted up again, the other children have
stopped jumping and are watching the funny new girl with
astonishment. She senses that her grandmother will secretly have
to wash her wet panties again. She shuts her eyes and jumps. She
feels no triumph.

Just a few years later the girl jumps from the highest
springboard of the public swimming pool, over and over, ignoring
every prohibition. Since she is technically inept, she hurts herself
badly every time. (This happens before everyone realizes that the
sign at the entrance, "No dogs and Jews," applies to her as well.)

NATURALLY THE MOTHER NEVER USED THE STEP-
father's pan-German first name. He became "Reinhold"—the name
came from a story titled "Little Reinhold." The girl did not know
the story, but was enchanted by the name: *"rein"* and *"hold,"* "pure"
and "gracious." She understood that Reinhold belonged to a breed
of humanity that was different from herself, from the mother, the
grandmother, different even from the uncle. What this difference
was she would not have been able to say, but it filled her with anx-
ious delight.

The man's way of playing "lion" with the girl—there
was something new, wild, and frightening in this, but it was also
soft and shiny like a lion's fur. They crawled around on all fours,
and the girl quailed at his very convincing imitation of a lion's roar,
enjoying her terror and its dissolution in the fearful lion's gentle
embrace. This man whom the girl was supposed to call "father" had
a soft and loving tenderness which the mother lacked. The mother's
caresses were vehement, stormy, and greedy. They resembled the
way she bathed her small children, the girl's half sisters. With burning zeal she would scrub the wildly screaming children, nearly skin-
ning them in the process, and then with a proud laugh present the
round, rosy bundles all wrapped up in bath sheets with little white
hoods to whatever onlookers were at hand.

There were other games too, games the parents played together, in which the girl's role, half observer, half participant, was less clearly defined. There was an exciting secrecy here; without any admonition, the girl was quite aware that these games were not to be mentioned outside the parents' room. Under this condition, she was occasionally granted a brief glance into an enchanted world, where man and wife were dressed in black velvet suits, the man wearing knee-length trousers, with thin white silk stockings on his shapely legs and black patent leather shoes with stiff tafetta roses on his slender feet. Both of them wore makeup. Who was who, and what was what? She felt as if she were treading on the wavering ground of a bog, lured by shifting will-o'-the-wisps, where you had to move cautiously and beware of taking a wrong step. It recalled the old fairy tale about the girl who was summoned to the king's palace and told to come neither on foot nor by carriage and neither clothed nor naked. Just as the girl herself was neither woman nor man but just a first intimation, a hint of a promise, and therefore just right for the part of the page in their game.

Occasionally the game took on a less refined and subtle form. The man would tie a bandana around his head, paint his cheeks red, and pretend to be "Hesse-Trinche," a peasant girl from his homeland in Hessia. Hesse-Trinche would cry and lament in her dialect: *"Ach Gottche, sprach's Lottche, was fang ich nur an, sieben Kinder und kein Mann!"*—"Oh Lordie, said Lottie, oh what shall I do, seven children and no husband!" The mother bent double with laughter over this holy simplicity, but the girl didn't like this game.

WHEN WAS IT THAT THE STEPFATHER, THE FATHER, Reinhold, the man, began to beat her? And why? Like so much else, it was impossible to remember, too difficult and too painful. But she feels the man's helpless, desperate fury when his fists hail down on her as she lies on the floor, trying to protect herself as best she can.

Somewhere deep inside she knows that it is she herself who has driven him to this outburst, this explosion of unrelieved emotions, this violation. The actual offense, a failure to do her homework, a tear in her dress, or rebelliousness of a general sort, serves only as a pretext. The real crime and the real guilt are not these, are not hers at all. It is from his own body that the man is attempting to drive out the devil—but the devil is stronger. The girl knows it and senses it, and though afterwards she locks herself in the bathroom to cry, though she flees to the kitchen, where she can always count on the servants' pity, though she allows the grand-mother to console her with sweets, she is conscious of her strength and is secretly proud of the power she imagines is hers.

She is his *"törichte Barbe,"* his "silly Barbie." The pet name was given the girl when she congratulated Reinhold with a poem for his birthday. The whole thing had been the mother's idea, it was she who chose the poem and filled the wicker basket with mar-zipan strawberries (as props). The poem is about a young girl who sets out in the morning to gather wild strawberries for her beloved. With lyrical expressions and a melting tone of voice she breathlessly praises his qualities, mental and physical. Not until the last line of the poem does one learn the identity of the man who is the object of this adoration: it is her father; and he always called her *"meine törichte Barbe."*

9

MEN WHO HIT. IN SELF-DEFENSE, AS PROTECTION against themselves, or to kill.

It happened during the transports that were later called "death marches" by others; those who were there did not call them that, not then, they just died.

The cattle car is supposed to hold so and so many men and so and so many horses, but no one has figured out how many women, or rather how many skeletons can be loaded into it.

But there are many, far more than anyone would have thought possible. The girl has succeeded, God alone knows how, to garner herself a seat in a corner. There she squats, her pointed knees drawn up to her chin. She won't move from this spot. Not even at those rare opportunities when the water soup is dispensed does she leave her place, which would have been pointless in any case, since someone has stolen her bowl, and she can't very well hold the soup with her bare hands. She is no longer suffering from hunger, only sometimes from thirst, and that is worse. She has reached a state of weightlessness, as if floating, drifting along on the fever waves of tuberculosis, clinging now and again to particular images and lines of poetry like a drowning person clutching at driftwood.

> *Ganz in Hauch gelöster Hades*
> *wenn einst Blatt um Blatt*
> *fällt, und an dem Ziel des Pfades*
> *Krümmung und der Schwung des Rades*
> *endlich Ruhe hat.*

> Hades utterly released in breath
> when at last leaf after leaf
> falls, and at the goal of the path
> the curve and sweep of the wheel come
> finally to rest.

She feels the falling of velvety leaves, one after the other. She feels the wheel gradually, gently slowing down; any moment it will stand still, utterly still. The mother's song about the rose lulls the girl to rest and forgetting. The rose, the heavy, fragrant, earthly rose in the garden at Berlin-Eichkamp, and the heavenly rose, the emblem of the Virgin Mary, who crushes the head of the snake beneath her silken shoe. "Death, where is thy sting, Hell, where is thy victory!"

As long as the girl stayed within the protective sphere of the mother's incantations, she felt no serious threat. Death no

longer frightened her. To die meant to be released from one's
mission, to come home. Forever. She knew this well, but sometimes
it happened that she forgot her knowledge and became one of
the foolish virgins and was cast out into the freezing cold and
darkness—into reality.

On this day they were let out of the freight cars and
permitted to stretch their stiff limbs on the frozen grass of the
large meadow. Was it an air raid or a problem with the locomotive?
Not that it mattered one way or the other, it was a brief respite, a
moment of grace, almost of happiness. To stretch your limbs, to walk
a few steps, to taste the cool, pure air, savor it, and absorb what
little warmth the pale winter sun could shed. Hundreds of women,
guarded by SS men, assisted by young soldiers—pilots without
planes, someone had said—who were standing guard at the
edge of the forest.

The girl went to them. Maybe, she thought, one of
them is from Berlin. Someone who could confirm her existence,
someone who would take notice of her the way Anna had taken
notice of her, someone who would understand that she wasn't just
"Prisoner A 3709," which of course she was too, but still, still she
was also Cordelia, Dela, the girl from Berlin-Eichkamp. She started
a conversation with a boy whose round face under the gray uniform
cap became more and more blank as he listened to the girl's quiet
tale. In answer and to console her he gave her half an onion and
a crust of bread and promised to share his meal ration with her if
she came back later. At one point, when the girl looked back at the
train, it seemed to her that one of the SS men was peering through
his field glasses in her direction. She knew what that meant, but
couldn't give it any heed. Someone was listening to her, someone was talking to her, she couldn't tear herself away.

And then the man is on top of her. Shouting and
hitting and hitting. The girl knows with paralyzing certainty that
he will beat her to death, that this is the end. The young soldier
watches in horror, then tries to stop the SS man, who, startled and

25

furious, starts venting his rage on him. Now the girl awakes from the nightmare, a last spark of the will to live flares up, perhaps because someone is standing up for her, she runs, even has the presence of mind to snatch up the gray coat on which she was sitting, and dashes toward the train. Like a rabbit (a squirrel) she runs in a zigzag course among the women who are sitting or lying in the yellow grass in the cold, pale, early spring light.

Someone trips her, others point and call with resounding voices: There she is! Here! But the girl reaches the train and never again leaves the freight car.

MEN WHO HIT.

He is a thin, tired, middle-aged man, a man with tormented eyes. His uniform hangs loose and sloppy on his frame, as if it belonged to someone else. The way he handles his rifle looks awkward; no doubt he is more accustomed to handling a pitchfork or a jack. He is one of those who were drafted when the war was already lost, a loser.

He sits by the door of the freight car, guarding it, more as a symbol than out of necessity. None of these women has the strength or even the desire to think of running away, and where would they run to if they did? Most of the time he just sits there, collapsed in his own hopelessness—is it he who guards them, or is it they who have him in their power?

The girl senses that he does not wish them ill. A few times he goes off to fetch water and gives them to drink. Then one day he comes dragging a large box containing little bags filled with sugar, the kind you are served in a restaurant—who knows where he dug them up. He tries to distribute them fairly, every prisoner is to get one bag of sugar, but the women go crazy and find unsuspected reserves of strength. They scream, hit, kick, pulling and tearing at the thin paper bags, so that the precious sugar runs through their clawing fingers. Desperately, the man shouts at them, urging

them to calm down, there is enough for everyone, but no one
listens to him.

And then he begins to hit. He does it out of horror,
out of disappointment and helplessness, he strikes into the midst
of this raving sea of suffering that threatens to devour him. The
cracking sound as the rifle butt pounds against bones that are
unprotected by layers of fat, the women's screams turning into
whimpers and groans. Then it is quiet. The women huddle
together, licking their wounds and whatever grains of sugar are
still to be found.

For the rest of the trip, the man sits collapsed in himself at his post by the door, emptied of all emotion. Every once in a
while he mumbles absently: "Oh Lord, oh my God." Is this what pity
looks like, the girl asked herself. Is this compassion?

10

THE GIRL NOW HAD A FATHER, AND HER STIGMA HAD
been removed, extinguished—so they claimed. But when she read
a novel in which the subject of lepers came up, she desperately
searched the palms of her hands for weeks and months. She thought
she had discovered in her hand the little white spot which, according to the novel, was the first sign of the sickness that would con-
demn its victim to be one of the hated and feared "impure" ones,
cast out of human society. She knew that something was wrong,
irrevocably wrong. But now that the family sat in their cozy squirrel nest playing house, now that the girl had started school and was
supposed to be a child among other children, now she was finding
it hard to maintain her sense of being special, being chosen. Her
mother didn't need her, not the way she used to, and if she had any
use for her at all, it was as an extra in the play she was staging now,

the story of the holy family, in which the girl was given the part of the innocent, ignorant child. But the girl was neither innocent nor ignorant, no child is, and she even less than others. The girls in her class gave her the nickname "snake," they sensed that the girl possessed a dangerous knowledge they lacked, and that she was capable of beguiling or enticing them into sin.

The girl was torn between the pride of being "different," a pride that was becoming more and more questionable, and the hopeless desire to belong, to be "like all the others." It was in fact, literally, hopeless—as on that day when she wanted so much to join the *"Bund deutscher Mädchen"* ("Union of German Girls").

A young BDM leader had come into the classroom. Proud, slim, and slender, she stood before the children in her brown uniform, a heavy knot of blond hair at the back of her neck, her eyes shining with enthusiasm. She spoke to the eight- to nine-year-olds about the joy of working for a common goal, for the good of the fatherland, spoke of high ideals, purity, and willing sacrifice. Surely there was no child in that classroom who took in those words with a more eager readiness than the girl. It was no doubt especially the call for sacrifice that appealed to her deepest instincts. Sacrifice comes before transformation, it is its indispensable precondition. Afterwards you might even become pure, slim, and slender, blond and blue-eyed.

The girl had received a new vocation. Shining with joy, she hurried home to inform her parents of her decision to join the BDM. Their answer was curt and clear: "Don't even think about it!" The girl began to beg and to argue, her mother and stepfather got angry, but in a different, more incomprehensible way than usual. Finally the girl lay on the couch in her mother's room, crying loudly; this time she wouldn't hide her despair, this time she could proclaim it, for it was justified and legitimate. This time it wasn't her fault, all she wanted this time was to be just like all the others, only more so ("but all the others can join" had been her strongest argument), and now she wasn't allowed to. The girl felt helplessly confused. All exits were barred. Here she was volunteering to be one of the rank and file, disciplined, advancing toward the goal and marching to the beat (*links, zwei, drei, vier, links*), and they wouldn't let her; but when she kept to herself as she usually did, observing, keeping her distance, they would say: "Why can't you join the other children, why can't you be like them!" Whatever she did was wrong, because there was something wrong with her, incurably wrong.

But she could still find consolation and even hope in fairy tales, in particular lines of poetry, and especially in the Mass. In all these the girl sought and found the same miracle and the same revelation: the miracle of transformation, the frog who turns into a prince, and "Lord, I am not worthy ... yet say but a word, and my soul becomes whole." That this phrase was said in Latin made the invocation all the more solemn and impressive. The purifying miracle of confession allowed her, at least for a while, to enjoy the liberating conviction that the the sign of the outcast, the mark of Cain, the leprosy itself had been truly and verily obliterated.

But there came a day when the girl did not dare to confess to her usual Father Confessor, the family's spiritual advisor, Father K. This gentle, simple, and in the eyes of the girl very old man was, by virtue of his office, the only one who could influence the mother to accept guidance, to give up some fixed idea, to make this or that concession to a reality she never saw. The mother revered him not only for his office but for who he was. In her life, he played the part of a good, strong, insightful guide (Virgil leading Dante through hell). The fact that Father K.'s office, age, and long years of habit had rendered him remarkably sexless probably contributed a great deal to the high esteem in which she held him.

No, this time the girl did not dare go to Father K. Her offense, or more precisely the consequences her sin would surely entail, were too terrible. But then whom could she turn to,

whom could she trust? At the same time it was so desperately important to be allowed to confess, to receive absolution. The punishment
would come without fail, but it would be easier to bear. Of course
she knew that the seal of confession was inviolable, that the priest's
pledge of secrecy was sacrosanct ... and yet. She trusted Father K.,
but she felt too ashamed in his presence. Confused and afraid, with
a cramp in her stomach, the girl wandered through streets where
she had never been, as far as possible from the district where her
family lived. She went in and out of several churches, trying to
catch a glimpse of the priest who went into the confession booth
when someone rang the little bell. Would she dare to entrust her
secret to him, could she trust him?

     Again and again the girl relived the scene in the
school courtyard. She no longer knows how the fight began, but
the other girls are standing around her in a circle, mocking her.
She doesn't care, she knows how to defend herself and pay them
back—with words. But then one of them says something about her
mother, calling her a "paint box." (Of course, "A German woman
does not smoke or paint her face." Her mother does both, and the
neighbors probably suspect the mother of not being as "German,"
meaning as Aryan, as one ought to be.)

     This insult of her mother is something the girl can-
not let pass. Her beautiful mother! The other mothers are cows
compared to her! Now she'll let them have it, she'll stuff their
mouths, and a little of the honor will—she hopes—reflect on the
girl as well. And so the words burst out of her: "But *my* mother is
in all the newspapers, she's the one who writes the ads for Uralt
Lavendel." (Uralt Lavendel was a well known eau de cologne.)
The moment these words are spoken, the girl feels like the wife of
Lot when she turned around. This was irrevocable, she knew it.
The other children of course did not seem to react very strongly,
they weren't even noticeably impressed, but the girl was sure that
they were only waiting for the right moment. The punishment

would come, the terrible punishment, and would not only come
to her—that would still be fortunate—it would also destroy her
mother, her stepfather, her grandmother, and her uncle—the whole
family. And it would be her fault and no one else's.

Two things had been impressed on the girl again and
again: "Don't tell anyone, ever, what Grandmother thinks of Hitler!"
And when she discovered through an unfortunate coincidence that
her mother wrote the advertising copy for Uralt Lavendel: "Don't
talk about that either, ever, not with anyone!" If she broke these
rules, she was told, some terrible, unspecified misfortune would
befall the whole family.

That the nasty things her grandmother said about
the Führer were better kept secret was something she could more
or less understand. After all, Grandmother was old and didn't
know any better; but the girl herself proudly remembered the day
when one of the maids took her to see the parade in honor of the
Führer's birthday. Some nice SA men lifted her up and passed her
to the front row, perhaps recalling the words "Let the little children come to me," and when the Führer's car drove past, the girl
threw a bouquet of violets in his direction. At that moment of
rapture it seemed to her that the Führer was smiling especially at
her. (Later, much later, this too would be dutifully registered in
the account of her debts.)

But the second prohibition the girl did not understand at all. No one had explained to her that her mother was a
"half-Jew" and therefore, of course, excluded from the *Reichs-
schrifttumskammer*, the state-appointed literary guild. Nothing,
not a word she wrote was allowed to be published and printed,
not even a few lines of advertising copy. Friends who were aware
of the family's financial difficulties, due in large part to the mother's
generous and spendthrifty nature, took pity and procured her the
ad writing job. But of course this could only be done in the greatest
secrecy.

For days the girl's fear gnawed and tore at her heart, like the little fox at the breast of the Spartan boy who kept it hidden under his shirt. At last she found a priest who took the heavy burden off her soul. The five "Ave Marias" he gave her for penance were full of relief and grateful rejoicing.

II

AROUND THIS TIME—THE GIRL WAS ABOUT NINE—SHE was invited to the first ball of her life. A relative on her grandmother's side was marrying off his daughter, and since the father of the bride was a high-ranking SS officer, the wedding turned into a costly affair, a sumptuous banquet with dancing.

Why did the mother accept this invitation? The stepfather, the tall, blond, archetypal "Aryan," wanted to decline it, and the girl was afraid she would miss all the glory, including her new, long dress made of heavy rose silk. But the mother insisted on the family's participating in the wedding feast, and as usual, her will prevailed. What were her unspoken intentions? Was it the half-conscious, magical idea of protecting the daughter by leading her directly into the wolf's den? Of presenting this girl, with her precocious charm and her vague, penumbral, seductive promise, with an implicit plea for mercy? "Just look at her, gentlemen (and help yourselves?), just look at her, surely you wouldn't want to harm this child? Perhaps you could use her as a little mascot, for protection against the evil eye, isn't she perfect for that? But please don't harm her!" Was that it? Or was it once again no more than the mother's obtuseness and lack of insight into a reality that would not be manipulated or conjured away—not even by Elisabeth Langgässer?

The girl never learned the mother's motive, but either way it would have sprung from the same source. At this source, the daughter, too, quenched her thirst, for good and for ill, for life and for death.

At this time a photograph is taken of the girl in her ball gown. She is sitting on a stool, straight as a candle, and her gaze beneath the strong, straight eyebrows encloses her solitude and her secrets. "Oh how good that no one knows that Rumpelstiltskin is my name!" No, no one knew anything, not even herself. But all of them were busy supposing, hissing and whispering, preparing the magic potion, stringing the net in which she would be caught. She looks and listens and has no words, only her dread of what she knows and yet does not know.

For weeks the girl dreamed and fantasized about the ball and the dress, which was designed especially for her. The material felt so soft and so heavy, the little dots woven into it glittered like jewels, her new patent-leather shoes gleamed and shone. How fine she would look!

She is almost blinded by the strong light of the ballroom and the hard colors, red and black, the swastika flags draped on the walls, the men's shining black SS uniforms. The girl feels the familiar, painful cramp of fear in her stomach, but at the same time she is wildly excited. This is how it must feel, exactly like this, when you've been invited to the witches' ball on Walpurgis Night! Her cavalier, the SS man who dances with her, lifts her high, high in the air and swings her round and round—it is a dizzyingly wonderful and at the same time terrifying feeling. She is completely at his mercy and wants it that way. Precisely at that moment it happens, the girl feels something in her panties, and it isn't just wetness, apparently she has diarrhea. Just don't let anyone notice, just don't let anyone smell it! (Smell the accident in her panties or the "filthy Jewish brat"?)

THE SAME STRONG, GLARING LIGHT. "*SELEKTION*" IN Auschwitz-Birkenau. Today the women from the weaving workshop are to be sorted, she has heard. Who is still fit for another month or two of work, and who's ready for the gas?

The girl has been ordered to work in the "office," a privileged position. Her chances for survival are unusually good, no brutally hard labor, sometimes an extra bowl of soup, and in addition the privilege of having a face which the SS women recognize—she's "the kid from Berlin" for them. Gerda, the block elder in the office, even has a bed of her own behind a partition. The bed is covered with a quilt and a lace coverlet. Sometimes the girl secretly looks at the rosy sheen of the quilt, it is so beautiful.

All this comes at a price, of course. The women in the office are, among other things, the personal servants of the SS guards and have small private errands to perform. This creates a bond between them, a relationship, no problem as far as the SS women are concerned, but full of shame and guilt on the part of the prisoners. At the same time they experience a bitter triumph in this place: the women of the office have discovered a method of tricking death for a month, for a week, for a day. They have acquired names and faces, and their particular abilities are known to the guards and are valued. There are women here, for instance, who can draw magnificent personal greeting cards. The girl especially likes a card in which a stork comes flying along with a baby cheerfully swinging in a diaper the stork is holding in its long red beak. A baby in Auschwitz.

Later the girl learns that the precisely measured dosage of gas is sufficient to kill adults, but that occasionally infants are still found alive when the floors of the gas chambers are tilted down—toward the fires of the crematorium. The girl is reminded of baked apples.

Part of the price that has to be paid is being forced to attend Dr. Mengele's selections within the camp and writing down the numbers of those who are going to be gassed. No names, just numbers. There are long shelves in the office bearing black oil-cloth ledgers full of numbers. Behind almost every number there is

a cross. A red cross for a "natural" death, a black one for the gas—
or maybe it was the other way around. When the girl was shoved
through the gate with the inscription *"Arbeit macht frei,"* the numbers had already become so high that there was no room left on the
prisoners' lower arms. And yet most of the new arrivals had already
been sorted in front of the trains and needed neither name nor number. So they started again from the beginning, putting an A in front
of the number. The girl became A 3709. Later she looked up 3709 in
the black oil-cloth ledger and found a cross behind the number.
The girl believed she knew a lot about her numerical sister, everything that was important to know. She had been a woman, the
triangle before the number indicated that she was a Jew; Jews,
"anti-social elements," Jehovah's Witnesses, and political prisoners
had variously colored triangles. She had been young and childless.
An older woman or a woman with a child in her arm or at her hand
would have been "sorted out" at the train. She was dead.

But the girl lived and bore her number, and this
number became a link between them, a bond of blood. 3709 would
not be forgotten, not be completely extinguished, as long as A 3709
still managed, however tenuously, to live and to breathe. From now
on the girl's life would never again be hers alone. Another woman
partook in it, "now and in the hour of our death."

The selection in the strong, glaring light in the
empty barrack. The screams, the crying, the cracking sound when
the bludgeons of the female SS guards hail down on the slack,
yellowish-white skin of the naked bodies; skin that appears to be
casually, almost accidentally draped over the frame of bones. The
bodies are already marked by death and evince the most complete
hopelessness, and yet often, against all probability, a last spark
of the will to live flares up in them. Again and again the inmates
examined by Mengele, weighed by his passionless gaze, found
too light and relegated to the "wrong" side of the barrack, make
desperate attempts to sneak back and hide among those who have
passed the test.

35

Mengele stands unmoved in the middle of the room as if on an island. He does not shout and he does not hit, his uniform is impeccable, his boots gleam. The girl is reminded of her first ball, of the SS man who whirled her around, higher, higher, faster, faster. She is overcome by the same submissiveness, the same terror and irresistible lure. She cannot and must not feel anything else, it is her job to write down the numbers as precisely and neatly as possible. She does not look into the eyes of the condemned, she sees only the numbers on their arms. A new arm, the slack, wrinkled skin of an old woman. A whining, begging voice: "Please, dear Miss, write that my husband was Aryan, pure Aryan!" The girl looks up and sees; sees the face of her grandmother.

Of course it can't be her grandmother, she died several years ago, "fortified by the holy last rites," at home in the squirrel nest. And yet, as the girl neatly records the number, she knows it is her own grandmother she is murdering. Is Mengele watching her? Is her mother watching her? Whose business is she conducting here anyway?

12

THE LADYBUG, SMOOTH AND ROUND, SHINING ON the juicy green leaf of grass. A ladybug in the month of May. Gently the girl stretches out her index finger, and the ladybug trustingly continues its walk from the leaf of grass to the girl's devoutly waiting finger. She counts the little black dots. The number of dots is the number of years she has to live. Multiply by ten if you want, but she doesn't want to. Carefully she breathes on the wings of the ladybug and, devoutly if out of tune, hums the old children's song:

Flieg, Käfer, flieg
Dein Vater ist im Krieg

Dein' Mutter ist in Pommerland
Pommerland ist abgebrannt
Flieg, Käfer, flieg!

Ladybug, fly
Your father's off to war
Your mother is in Pomerania
Pomerania's all burned down
Ladybug, fly!

A secret and sacred bond has been forged between the child and
the ladybug, the song is the password. The two of them understand
each other and know what they speak of—already back then. The
unreachable father, far away at war, and the mother in the desolate,
charred land. But a human breath brushes your wings, and you
fly, small and round you fly toward the sun. Away from longing,
sorrow and pain, from loneliness and abandonment, your wings
carry you—toward the sun, toward death and beyond. But you
fly. Ladybug, fly!

13

DATES AND EVENTS BLEND INTO EACH OTHER,
reality becomes more and more confused, intangible and chaotic,
but here and there a clue offers itself, a milestone, a sharply out-
lined memory.

The girl has just entered secondary school, so she
must be ten years old. Her classmates have thought up a new kind
of mischief: letting the air out of other students' bicycle tires. Naturally the girl wants to be part of it; it seems a sure ticket to "being
like the others"! Or maybe not? She knows very well that when she
deflates a tire, it isn't just a harmless little joke; as she hears the air

hissing and the tube becomes a slack, flattened thing, she feels a mean, deeply gratifying, vengeful satisfaction. That is probably why, of all the girls, she is the one who is caught in the act and brought before the principal, who informs her that due to her bad behavior she will be expelled from the school. No tears, no begging helps; and yet the principal doesn't seem angry at all, on the contrary, she looks at the girl with pitying eyes. Nevertheless the girl feels rebellious. The punishment bears no relationship to her offense, and why her, why always her? She is afraid of going home, and wanders, wavering, through the streets, for hours. Oh, these Berlin streets! Streets—fear, fear—streets. When she finally dares to come home and, stammering and apologizing, tries to confess her shame and disgrace, the parents already seem to know —and not to care. "All right, all right, go to the kitchen now and get yourself something to eat!" The girl doesn't know what is worse: to be severely punished, even to get a beating, or this lenience which is so indifferent. Why would they let her get away so lightly? It can't be. The punishment will surely follow, and it will be all the more severe.

She can't possibly know that the whole thing is a charade, a farce, prearranged with the best intentions between the parents and the principal. The girl has been attending secondary school for a few months, and now it has been determined that she cannot show the *"Ariernachweis,"* the proof of Aryan origin that is the prerequisite for the enjoyment of a higher education. The principal has no choice, the girl has to leave the school, but since she is a compassionate woman, she yields to the parents' pleas and invents a subterfuge for the girl's expulsion. To spare her feelings, she will be kept ignorant for as long as possible.

Besides, how could anyone explain it to her, where would one begin? Later, when it becomes unavoidable, the stepfather takes on the delicate task of explanation. "If you are a Jew," he said, "then I am a Jew as well, we are all descendants of father Abraham, we all have our roots in the Covenant. In this sense, we Christians are all Jews." But at that point the girl already knows that this is not true, that it is not her truth.

14

THE FOG THICKENS AROUND THE GIRL. FOR THE time being she still lives in the seemingly sheltered world of the squirrel nest, but she has a dark sense that she is just a guest and a stranger there. The little sisters arrive one by one, and the grandmother and the uncle still live on the top floor, the grandmother steadily getting weaker, the uncle amiably evasive as always. He lets himself be devoured by his—top secret—work as chief engineer at Siemens, he fusses and tinkers with his car and devotes himself to his great hobby, photography. Faithfully he portrays the growing family which now extends from the ground floor through the entire little house. The girl has a room of her own, a garret with a slanted ceiling. She spends hours kneeling before the oval window, gazing out at the neighbors' well-tended little gardens. She wants to stretch out her hands and beg God to preserve and protect this modest idyll. She senses that it is endangered, feels it in her own body, hears the ticking of death's clock. Already now, she sees her uncle's photographs as documents and mementos which you mark with a little cross, like a postcard from a vacation: This is where my house was. Here is where I lived. Remember me!

In their little garden stands a large cherry tree. The girl carved a heart with her initials and those of the neighbor's boy into its bark. The knife slipped and she cut her wrist. The little scar next to the artery became the seal of her belonging, the warrant and proof that she too has a homesteader's rights in the world of life. Later the mark of Auschwitz would be tattooed on the same arm, but each time she lovingly looked at this little scar, even much later as an adult woman, she was reminded and reassured that the mark of Auschwitz is not the only truth about her and her life. Even though it is the greatest and deepest of all—for don't death, pain, and suffering always have the last word?—it is not the only truth.

Among the details of this good little world of life, which the girl did not regard as her rightful inheritance but gratefully accepted as a gift, was the scent of freshly baked cake waiting on a Sunday morning under white napkins for the family's return from Mass. The girl, with the missal already in her hand, never failed gingerly to lift the napkins in order to see what kind of cake they would have this Sunday: crumb cake with lots of sweet crumbs and a thin crust, plum cake, or cheese cake. After church the pleasure of eating would be doubled, because it seemed so well deserved. Holy communion for the soul and crumb cake for the body—at such moments the world was whole and the girl a part of it.

This kind of happiness, complete and infinite as an egg in the palm of a hand, came to the girl most palpably at Easter time. The mysteries of death and resurrection became a tangible and real presence in the drama of the Easter Mass, which culminates in the overwhelming, exultant transcendence of Easter. Light, but a different kind of light, the altogether different, the living light after the dark night of death, the bells tumbling all over each other in their eagerness to proclaim that miracle of great joy, the resounding surge of the organ, and the jubilant choir: for the girl, all this became her own death and her own resurrection. As, no doubt, it was meant to be. "For if we be dead with Him, we shall also live with Him."

Easter was also the spring sun, easter eggs hidden among crocuses, easter lilies and tulips in the garden, the first white knee-socks of the year, and Goethe's Easter Song: *Vom Eise befreit sind Strom und Bäche...*"—"released from ice are river and streams..." This intoxicating liberation, this unchecked rush of gurgling, bubbling joy was everywhere, all around the girl and within herself. Her armor, the stiff supporting corset of hardness and callousness, had melted and dissolved, she dared to open up, to be soft and yielding. For a while.

15

WHEN THE JEWISH STAR CAME ... THAT SOUNDS like "when school began" or "when autumn started," so matter-of-fact and perfectly undramatic, just one of those things. Isn't there another way to say it, are there no other words? No, not for the girl, the *Judenstern* was just one of those incomprehensible things that turned the ground under her feet into a wavering bog, but which at the same time she accepted as natural and unavoidable. She had learned that anything can happen, no matter what and no matter when, and for inexplicable reasons.

There is, however, one clear image from that time. The girl has just come home from school, she has been going to a Jewish school for the past several months (how was that explained?), she is sitting at the kitchen table while the mother is preparing her meal. It is the girl who is telling the mother about the *Judenstern*, she must have heard about it in school, the mother cries out and very nearly drops the frying pan she has just lifted off the stove. The girl observes her with cool disapproval: What's so bad about that, why get hysterical over something like this? The girl herself assumed that her fog-shrouded world, felt-gray with blurred contours, would be brightened by the yellow Jewish star. For a while now she hasn't been allowed to sleep at home. She travels to school from the place where she sleeps, comes home to the squirrel nest after school, and returns to her sleeping quarters in the evening.

Now that she wears the *Judenstern*, she will have to leave home for good. She realizes that she has become a mortal threat to the entire family. The young cuckoo must be thrown out of the nest. Every house and every apartment where a Jew lives must be marked with a Jewish star made of paper and pasted to the door. That simplifies matters when the gray, canvas-topped trucks come to gather their harvest. The girl quickly learns to spot them. Carefully she peers around the corner before she ducks into a new street. Streets—fear. Fear—streets.

Like the leper's little bell, the Jewish star on the door warns against the plague with which the girl is infected.

16

AT THE SAME TIME SHE IS ALSO FORCED TO LEAVE the Catholic Girls' Club, of which she is a member.

One evening she is invited to the home of the much admired leader of her chapter. She is very proud of the unusual honor. On the table are candles and cake, on the wall hangs the sentimental death mask of the "Unknown Girl found in the Seine" (a requisite in certain German adolescent girls' rooms), and on the chest of drawers stands an arts-and-crafts Madonna. It's all very atmospheric. Atmosphere is important in the Catholic Girls' Club. The young woman attends to the girl, is friendly and protective, like an older sister, and very embarrassed. The girl must understand, she says, it's very regrettable and it pains her greatly, but there is no choice. If the authorities should discover that there are members who wear the *Judenstern*, their chapter would be dissolved. So it's probably best if the girl stops coming to the meetings. "You know our motto: All for one and one for all."

For one dizzying second the girl wonders whether this might not be the time for "All for one," but she rejects this heretical thought right away. If someone is to be sacrificed, if someone has to leave the boat, then of course it is she—she, the elect, she, the chosen one. She accepts the leader's farewell gift, a picture of a saint, endures her tearful embrace and swallows back her own tears. But she never put the picture of the saint into her missal, as was the custom. At some point it got lost.

17

THE EVENING WALKS THROUGH THE STREETS OF Berlin, holding her stepfather's hand. She still occasionally stole her way home to the squirrel nest. When it started to get dark, her stepfather would accompany her on the long walk back to the place where she was presently being put up. Since Jews are not permitted to use public transportation, they have to walk. To keep pace with the tall man, the girl is almost forced to run. He did not talk to her, but she felt his grim rage, his mute, helpless wrath at those who wanted to harm his little girl, his *"törichte Barbe."*

On these walks the girl felt a strange security. The man's great, wordless wrath was her shield and protection.

18

BERLIN IS BEING EMPTIED, "CLEANSED" OF ITS STILL remaining Jews, and the girl is being shoved from one place to another, wherever there's still someone living behind the marked doors. For a while she sleeps in what used to be called the "gentlemen's room"—on the wall Böcklin's "Sin" in voluptuous and fear-inspiring enticement, and a curtain of beads separating her room from the bedroom of the mistress of the house. The girl lies awake until late at night listening to the confusing and frightening sounds behind the beaded curtain. The hopeless lamenting of the woman when she is alone, and the half suffocated laughing and moaning when one of her many male acquaintances is visiting her.

The woman's many attempts at suicide, on the other hand, don't alarm the girl greatly. She realizes that they are not meant in earnest, aren't really intended to lead to her death. The suicide attempts, always carried out with sleeping pills—the woman used to work as an assistant in a drugstore—, are something like acts of revenge against her absconded husband, the Aryan husband who abandoned his Jewish wife and took their only child, their son, with him. The wife-mother's bitterness and hatred of the faithless traitor are boundless, she rages and screams until she breaks down in exhaustion, weeping quietly over the photograph of her son.

LATER THE GIRL LIVES IN A BEDROOM THROUGH which a little Jewish seamstress has realized her dream of elegance and refinement. Everything is white, a gleaming, innocent white, decorated with golden, winding tendrils in art-nouveau style. It must have taken years to create all this splendor with needle and thread, even if, like this soft and plump Viennese woman, one has been sewing for "Berlin's most elegant ladies, actresses, and wives of professors and doctors." For her, this is more than just the furnishing of a bedroom, it is the visible sign and proof that she has achieved something in life. Others receive titles and diplomas for their ability and their pride; her prize was this bedroom. To leave this in order to save her life—that was impossible, this *was* her life.

Now she shares her bedroom and her life with the girl. The seamstress is one of the diminishing number of Jews who have not yet been taken away, for her talents are needed by the Wehr-macht now: she is sewing uniforms. One day she and the girl were almost "collected," but the seamstress was able to present a certificate proving that she was working for the Wehrmacht. The Gestapo man pointed at the girl: "And that one?" The seamstress replied quickly: "Oh, she helps me, she sews the buttonholes." The girl had never been able to sew a stitch, since her grandmother had always done her needlework assignments.

That was a lucky moment, but it wasn't likely to be repeated, they both knew that.

Not long after that came the night when they were awakened by loud footsteps and shouts in the vestibule. Suitcases and people being kicked downstairs: *"Los, los, schneller, fertig-machen . . ."* The girl and the seamstress lie quiet as mice in their white beds in the pitch-black room with its black air-raid curtains carefully drawn shut. It doesn't occur to either of them to turn on the light—as if it were possible to hide in the dark; and besides they are petrified. They know that at any moment the men will pound and kick at the door, at any second their turn could come. The girl is incapable of moving a finger, let alone fold her hands in prayer, but deep inside she prays to the Virgin of the protective mantle: "Blessed Mary, spread your mantle, make it our shield and protection."

Then suddenly it is still, completely still, and in the stillness they hear the truck starting in the street. A miracle had happened. The star on their door was perfectly visible, but the angel of death had passed. The Mother of God had concealed them under her sky-blue, star-studded coat, or perhaps it was the girl's mother who had used her magic powers to throw a cloak of invisibility over the daughter and her hostess. For the time was not yet. The girl was saved. For now.

19

SHORTLY THEREAFTER THE GIRL BECOMES CORDELIA Garcia-Scouvart, a Spaniard with a genuine Spanish passport,

Spanish citizenship, and a German residence permit stamped
into the passport.

The higher powers in her life—her mother and the
church—had torn her from the jaws of death—for the time being,
she has only been granted a brief deferment, but they don't know
that. The daughter's report about her night of terror got through to
the mother. Her protective images were blown away, shattered. Reality struck its claws into the mother, without, however, impairing her
faith in her own magical omnipotence, which would enable her to
save her daughter after all. Now she acted with the furious strength
and courage of a tigress whose young is in danger.

Not far from the church where the mother went to
Mass was a military hospital, and among the wounded German soldiers being treated were a few Spaniards from the symbolic army
Franco had sent Hitler, presumably a token of gratitude for his aid
during the civil war. The mother had noticed a young Spanish officer who regularly came to Mass; this good-looking and probably
pious young man, she decided, had to be her daughter's savior.

The girl was not at all surprised to hear that after just
one conversation with the mother, the young man had, on the spot,
offered to engage in a fictitious marriage with the girl, a marriage
that would provide her with Spanish citizenship. But since the
fourteen-year-old girl was not officially of marriageable age, the
plan failed; nor was an adoption possible, since the man was not
old enough for that. At any rate, it was he who put the mother in
touch with an ancient lady who lived in a castle near Munich.
Supposedly the old woman was the last Bavarian crown princess
and was herself a descendant of Spanish royalty—perhaps she
could help. The mother drove to Munich and found a helpless
old woman who lived in constant fear of her Nazi daughter-in-law,
a card-carrying member of the German Women's Federation. But
the mother also met the old woman's faithful Spanish servants, the
cook and the gardener, who declared themselves willing to adopt
and save the girl.

The fairy tale became true. After all the formalities
had been rushed to completion and the girl had been granted Spanish citizenship in a solemn ceremony at the Spanish embassy, she
was able to take off the yellow star. Then she was sent to the magic
castle, where the good queen was being held prisoner by the evil
witch. The girl was hidden in the room of the servants. One day
the witch drove off in her splendid carriage, equipped with many
horse-powers, and the girl was brought to the fairy-tale queen's
chamber. The girl curtsied and thanked her, and the fairy-tale
queen regarded her with her sad friendly eyes and blessed her
with the sign of the cross. After that the girl returned to the squirrel nest, for now she had the talisman that would protect her and
her family against all the powers of evil—the Spanish passport.

That evening, the mother celebrated the return of
her Proserpine from the valley of the shadow of death. "The circle
has closed," the mother said. The daughter, born in Munich amidst
pain and tears, had been born again, saved again, and had returned
again to the mother in the same city. Never had the girl found her
mother more beautiful than on that night. Her black hair and her
red mouth shone, the radiance of the burning candles was reflected
in the green goblets filled with golden-yellow wine. It was so beautiful that it hurt the girl. She would have liked to cry, because something told her that this was a farewell party, not a feast of reunion,
as the mother believed. The girl knew that she had been granted
only a brief reprieve, as an act of mercy, that Proserpine was only
a visitor among the living, and soon the hour would strike, the
hour of the wolf between night and dawn, the hour of the gray
underworld. On this shining, festive evening the girl took leave
of everything she loved. "I come once again now—and then
nevermore." Nevermore.

But there was something she would take with her
on her way. Ariadne's thread, which the mother had given her, the
thread of the fairy tale, the myth, and the poem, fine as silk and,
it was said, stronger than death. But the girl also knew that this

47

thread she had received from her mother, the unsevered umbilical
cord, would lead her where she did not want to go, to the gate
of the realm of the dead. She did not know yet what would await
her there, but she already sensed the last great solitude closing
in around her.

20

"WE WANT TO SAY GOOD-BYE TO DR. MICHAELIS." DR.
Michaelis had been recently chosen as the girl's guardian. Since she
was born out of wedlock, the law requires her to have a guardian,
and since she is of Jewish background—the requisite documents
have been assembled by now—the guardian has to be Jewish as
well. Dr. Michaelis, lawyer and head of a liberal Jewish congregation in Berlin, meets the requirements. He is a delicate, thin, very
cultivated and polite elderly genetleman. Now he is to be picked up
for transport, and the parents and the girl want to say good-bye.

In the stairway of the house in Charlottenburg where
Dr. Michaelis lives there is a smell of cabbage and dishwater. The yellow star on the door has been applied so neatly that Dr. Michaelis
must have used a yardstick to measure the distance between the
doorposts. The packed valises stand in the apartment, with printed
business cards serving as name tags. Frau Michaelis, a voluminous
woman, her face puffed from crying, is rummaging about, trying to
remember what items essential for their physical well-being she
might have forgotten to pack.

Her husband, on the other hand, is calm and col-
lected; when the guests arrive, he is carefully clipping his nails. The
bright summer light shines through his thin body. He is in the true
sense of the word "illuminated," the girl finds, almost like a spirit-
being, odorless, weightless, a candle flame that will be snuffed out
by the summer wind. "A gentle death"? No, in all probability not,

48

but it is conceivable, it is likely, that Dr. Michaelis offered no resistance, that he took a deep, deep breath and thus put out the flame himself, welcoming the darkness.

But now he is still standing by the window, shining and clipping his nails. When the guests are led in, he begs their forgiveness, he hadn't expected to see them so soon. But probably there wasn't much time left, he said, it was necessary to be ready and prepared. "You never know when you'll have another chance to clip your nails," he says with a faint smile. Then he gives the parents and the girl some souvenirs. Dr. Michaelis was a loving collector of beautiful, usually fragile things. The mother receives some coffee cups made of Meissen porcelain, adorned with shepherd girls playing on the pastures of innocence. The father receives an ebony cane with an ivory handle. "I am so glad that at least these objects aren't falling into rough hands," says Dr. Michaelis, urging them to accept the gifts. Then he turns to the girl: "I know you like to read Stifter, that's why I'm giving you this," and he strokes her head with his thin, bony hands, the hands of an old man. The girl receives two gold-edged, leather-bound volumes containing Adalbert Stifter's world of infinite peace, of time beyond time, an ocean of time for quiet living and thriving, for patience, attention, and imperceptible growth. The girl curtsies, says thank you, and looks at the floor. Then she notices Dr. Michaelis's little feet in the old-fashioned button-down boots. She tries to count the little black knobs, but she doesn't get to the end of them.

It is time to say good-bye to Dr. Michaelis.

21

IT HAD BEEN SUCH A BEAUTIFUL FALL DAY IN THE woods, *"im schönen deutschen Wald."* The girl and the uncle had driven there to gather mushrooms and berries, and in Uncle Heini's

---

company the girl could relax and rest. He wasn't constantly trying to impress something upon her, he made no demands, provoked no storms of emotion, all he offered was restful warmth and friendliness. Occasionally he even managed to surprise her with cryptic jokes and a half-stifled laugh.

When they came home with their harvest in the evening, they found a note on the kitchen table telling them to knock on the parents' door even if it was late. The girl immediately expected trouble: What had she done or failed to do this time? It had to be something serious, why else would they take her to task so late in the evening. Because obviously it was about her, about her failing, her fault. Had the little white spot in her hand not grown lately? It seemed to her that she could see the mark of leprosy more clearly when she locked herself in the bathroom to examine her stigma. Had anyone else seen it too? She pulled herself together, bracing herself for what she knew would come, had to come.

The mother and the stepfather were already lying on the broad sofa that served as a bed at night. Above the bed hung a more than three-foot-high figure of Christ, who, not having a cross, screamed out his naked suffering at the beautiful room with its few but carefully chosen pieces of furniture. The room also served the father as a studio during the rare hours when his dismal job and the mother's needs allowed him some time for a project to which he would have dearly loved to devote his life: writing a book about Saint Augustine. When Wilhelm Hoffmann, Ph.D., turned into the mother's Reinhold, he knew that he would be barred from any academic career in the future. That was his punishment for consciously desecrating the Aryan race. That his own family would ostracize him for many years was something he probably had not reckoned with, but in their eyes he had soiled the family's honor by marrying a woman with an illegitimate child.

The suffering Christ seemed to belong in Reinhold's room. This man's defense against the divers torments of life (to which eventually, sometimes for long periods, the mother would also contribute) consisted of silence, of sitting at his desk mute as a fish, unreachable, letting not a word pass his lips, stifling the cry of rage and despair that was pounding inside him and wanted out. This brooding could go on for days, filled to the brim with that dense, dull silence.

The wounded, pain-twisted body on the wall shared Reinhold's silence. Suffered with him.

The moment the girl stepped into the room, she searched the stepfather's face for a clue. The mother's behavior rarely gave any indication of the seriousness of the situation. Since she lacked any sense of proportion, she could be just as desperate and beside herself when the maid had given notice as when her best friend had committed suicide—at least for the moment. Just as she would take passionate delight in a new poem by Wilhelm Lehmann, she could go into raptures about her little daughter's drawings. It didn't even require a personal occasion for the mother to give dramatic vent to her emotions. It could happen that she would enter a room where the stepfather appeared to be scolding the girl, and immediately the mother would intervene by giving the daughter a resounding slap in the face. "But why are you hitting her?" the man would ask, dumbfounded. The mother was no less astonished by his question. "You're scolding her, aren't you?" she would reply in perfect candor.

The stepfather's outward behavior was comparatively easy to interpret. Jaws clenched with rage, tormented blue eyes staring into space, creases in the forehead, signs of a burning headache —all these could be seen now, and the girl knew. It had to be much worse than she had assumed.

Silently the mother handed her brother a typewritten letter on official stationery, a summons to Gestapo Headquarters. It concerned the girl, but the mother had already decided to accompany her daughter—as far as she could.

As always, the girl was very proud of her beautiful, elegant mother, who on this day was wearing a white linen coat and a

large black patent-leather handbag. However, the girl was frightened by the large gray house of the Gestapo's headquarters and the
echoing clatter of boots as SS men tramped up and down the broad
marble steps, it all reminded her of the dragon's cave. Mother and
daughter searched the long corridors for room number so-and-so.
But the moment they entered that room, the girl's fear vanished.
The official who had summoned them wasn't wearing a uniform,
he was a small, thin man with a thin moustache and glasses. Politely
he offered the mother a chair. The girl, however, had to stand while
he explained what the issue was. Yes, the problem was this: the girl
had a valid Spanish passport with a Spanish entry visa. This was,
from a German point of view, unobjectionable ("unfortunately," he
almost said, but then he realized that this was not necessary). The
fact of the matter, however, he went on, was that, in order to leave
the country, a German exit visa would be needed, and this would
certainly not be obtainable. "I see you are not wearing a *Judenstern*," he said, addressing the girl. It wasn't an accusation yet, just
a statement of fact. The girl noted with great satisfaction that he
had addressed her with "*Sie*," the polite form normally reserved for
adults. It was the first time she had ever been addressed that way;
evidently she was now considered an adult. Nevertheless it was the
mother who explained that at the Spanish embassy they had been
assured that as a Spanish citizen the girl was not subject to the German race laws and could therefore not be forced to wear the Jewish
star, in particular and additionally since she was born a Catholic.
"That may be so," the official patiently replied, "but," and again he
addressed the girl directly, "we have prepared a document here, for
which we request your signature." (Again he had said "*Sie*.") The
document turned out to be a statement made out in the name of the
girl, affirming that she accepted dual citizenship, German as well as
Spanish, and that furthermore she would voluntarily conform to
German laws, including the race laws and their particular applica-
tion to herself. Which would include the wearing of the *Judenstern*
and, possibly, a future "removal" to the East.

Uncertainly, the daughter looked at the mother, and her gaze met with a white mask in which the overly red mouth burned like a wound. No support could be expected from the mother at this moment, the girl immediately realized that. A great fear befell her, but as always, defiance came to her aid. Oh no, not so fast, and not the *Judenstern* again. "Removal to the East" didn't sound so good either, but she had had her experiences with the *Judenstern*. The girl decided to play "the cheeky Berlin girl," a part she had created on past occasions with considerable success. "May I please call my embassy," she said to the official, and found the sound of that quite grown-up and impressive—after all, he had addressed her with "*Sie*." There was a flash in the eyes behind the spectacles, and the moustache twitched with suppressed laughter: "Why, certainly, Miss, here is the telephone!" Obligingly he picked up the telephone and put it in front of her, and her hand was already on the receiver when he continued, and now the dragon spit fire: "*But*," and the word sounded like the crack of a whip, "*but* if you do not sign on the spot, we will have to prosecute your mother!" He told the girl that the mother had arranged the daughter's Spanish adoption in order to circumvent German laws, which could be regarded as a serious offense, as treason, high treason, and some third category which the girl was later unable to remember. However, if the girl signed now, no harm would be done, and the mother's lapse could be excused. "And," he added, just to be sure: "You are no doubt aware of the fact that your mother is a half-Jew."

Again the daughter looked at the mother and met with the gaze of her beautiful brown eyes, eyes that shone with intensity, that knew how to cast a spell on the girl, but which now were full to the brim with wordless, helpless pain. No one said anything, nothing needed to be said, there was no choice, there never had been, she was Cordelia, who kept her vow of fidelity, she was also Proserpine, she was the chosen one, and never had she felt closer to her mother's heart. Her voice was choked, but finally she got the words out: "Yes, I'll sign."

The dragon, sated and contented now, turned back into an almost friendly official. By way of a good-bye, he informed the girl: "And now you can go to the room across the hallway and pick up a new *Judenstern*. It costs 50 Pfennig."

22

WHEN THEY CAME TO PICK HER UP ONE MORNING, she ought to have been prepared, if not exactly willing. Nevertheless the girl cried, was afraid, didn't want to go.

The young "half-Jews" who were buying time and hoping they could buy their lives by doing the Gestapo's dirty work, treated the girl with care. Ordinarily they dragged people out of their beds, kicked them and beat them and yelled—out of despair or because they identified with the hangmen. With the girl it was different. They knew her. Not that she was one of them, but she was a part of their life, their lost innocence, which they would try to shelter and protect—for as long as possible. They treated her like their little sister, and the girl, who had always been the big sister, found the part agreeable. She had already been living with them for several months in the Jewish Hospital on Iranische Strasse, and she was sharing her bed with some of them. Definitely not for sensual pleasure, for the fourteen-year-old was not yet awake to the urgencies of sex, no prince had stirred her from her dreams and fantasies with a kiss. She was "late," had the merest suggestion of breasts, and had not menstruated yet.

What was it then, that tempted the girl? Was it the chance to be close to the power of the rulers, the victors, a closeness that would have to be paid with dark complicity, with damnation and disaster? Was it a kind of vertigo, the lure of a free fall, that impelled her to take the plunge with them, hand in hand? But brave little tin soldiers always fall into the fire, don't they?

For some reason all these young men were from
Cologne, and their pronounced Cologne dialect delighted the girl
with its mixture of brutality and playful tenderness. The brothers
Hans and Heinz both became the girl's bedmates. How different
they were! Hans was tall, dark, and handsome like a housemaid's
Casanova, a desperado with the Mother of God on a medallion
around his neck (all the boys were baptised). Hans was blond Greta's lover, and Greta, for her part, bought time by sharing Dr. Lustig's bed. Greta was chief nurse in the children's department, and
Dr. Lustig functioned as head of the hospital and was, according to
rumor, a henchman for the Gestapo. When Greta returned late at
night from Dr. Lustig's bed, she would proudly, but also disgust-
edly, show her hickies and black-and-blue marks; proudly because
every black-and-blue mark was the sign of a victory in the merciless
struggle for survival, a struggle that was acted out between herself
and another nurse who competed with Greta for Dr. Lustig's favors.
He had indicated to them that only one of them would escape being
taken away—in the end it was Greta. She tra-la-laed her loathing
away with German popular songs: "A man like that you don't forget,
and others you don't kiss." She dreamed, consoled, sang, and chat-
tered away her degradation with the memory and the story of the
great love of her life, a young Jewish doctor who had emigrated to
America before it was too late ... and others you don't kiss.

The girl observed, took part, and felt like an outsider.
She knew that she had left the squirrel nest forever, but in the world
of the Jewish Hospital there was no place for her, in this world, too,
she had no homesteader's right. She was treated kindly, sometimes
like a mascot or a talisman, but she didn't belong here, she didn't
belong anywhere. Her attempt to find a way into the world of the
damned and condemned via Hans's bed failed miserably. A few
days earlier, Hans had been wounded with a knife by one of the
Jews he was supposed to pick up, a man who had decided to fight
for his life. Hans wrestled him down and killed him. In the night
when the girl came to his bed, he was suffering greatly from his

wounds, and after a half-hearted, failed attempt he gave up. Relieved, he laughed good-naturedly: "No, girl, this may be God's finger, I guess it's not meant to be."

It was meant to be with his brother Heinz. Skinny, red-haired Heinz could be tearfully sentimental and suffered greatly from pangs of conscience. The girl consoled him as well as she could, but had only her body to offer. Secretly she felt contempt for the crybaby Heinz and admired Hans the fallen angel.

The Jewish Hospital in Berlin, a vestibule of hell. Here the Gestapo had swept together those remnants of Berlin Jewry who were still being spared for some reason or other: Jews with foreign citizenship, half-Jews who had not yet been "catalogued" as first- and second-degree half-breeds, people who were well known or famous outside Germany, men who had received a high decoration in World War I. But there were also some who were physically or mentally ill, like the woman in the closed ward on the first floor whose peacock cries rang across the courtyard every day without cease, and the pair of twins, Leah and Reah, who lay in the children's ward, quietly playing with the bars on their cribs. They were about a year old, but so mal- and undernourished that they could barely sit up. It was one of the girl's tasks to feed them with a gruel made of old bread crusts, and sometimes, though not often, Leah or Reah would smile at her. Then the girl would fleetingly think of her little sisters back home in the squirrel nest. The twins had been born at a time when all Jewish children had to have Jewish names, and Jews who had already been born were made to add the names Sarah or Israel to their given names. Cordelia Maria Sarah—someone had said that Sarah meant "queen," but the girl felt no pride.

Every day the Gestapo, the SS, and their stooges had some business with Dr. Lustig or the hospital. Among them was a beautiful young Jewish woman who was treated by everyone with fawning subservience because she was known to be a spy who made

a living by denouncing her neighbors. She sniffed out Jews who
had managed to hide or go underground and delivered them to the
Gestapo. One day the young woman's elegant, self-assured mask
cracked. She wanted to explain, she begged for understanding,
maybe even for forgiveness. In tears, she said that denouncing others
was the price she had to pay for keeping her aged parents out of
harm's way. The confession was superfluous and useless; in the Jewish Hospital in Berlin notions like guilt and atonement no longer
mattered, they had lost all content and meaning, but maybe, the girl
thought, maybe there could be something like mercy. Yes, surely there
was mercy, there had to be, she thought, and where else if not here?

In the meantime, what did matter was living and surviving—at any price. Everyone slept with everyone, all the medicine
cabinets were quickly emptied, the last supply of narcotics dwin-
dled away, there was a flourishing trade in black market cigarettes;
rumors and gossip ran unchecked through the "Jewish grapevine."
And you lived and survived until the next transport and the next
one after that . . . There was no need for any handwriting on the
wall, the signs were present every day, in flesh and blood and stone
and concrete. The black uniforms of the SS and the Gestapo's
trenchcoats were an always familiar, always newly terrifying sight
(will it be my turn next time?), and one of the hospital buildings
was used as a depot for Jews who had been "picked up" and were
going to leave with the next transport.

So now it was the girl's turn. It was Hans and Heinz
who led her, gently but firmly, up the stairs from the children's ward
to the closed ward, where the mentally ill, along with some others
slated for transport, were temporarily kept. Standing by the barred
window of the small locked room where she had been locked in, the
girl cried and called out, begging for someone to inform her parents, she wanted to say good-bye to them. The parents came on the
evening when the girl had already been brought to the building
from where the transport would leave in a few hours. By now she

had stopped crying. As a farewell gift, the mother gave her a small antique silver cross, which the girl sewed into the shoulder pads of her coat. Both the stepfather and the mother traced the sign of the cross on her forehead with their thumbs. To protect and preserve her—in this life or the next? The sign of sacrifice or of salvation? The girl did not know, but weren't sacrifice and salvation indissolubly linked, intertwined like twins in the womb, mingled like water and wine of the sacrament, like love and pain, life and death? But the girl knew one thing: Now there would be no return, now she was excluded forever, singled out, separate, and not set aside but chosen. This she wanted to believe.

Was this how the saints and martyrs felt when they sang as they climbed the pyre? But how did they deal with their trembling fear, their choking terror, their solitude and their help-less crying? They probably did as the girl did—they swallowed what had to be swallowed, in order to endow the meaningless with mean-ing. They learned to make a conscious act of submission, learned not to surrender and succumb to their fate, but to take it into their hands and make it their own. No one should be able to say later on: "In tears she was torn from her mother's arms and taken to There-sienstadt." No, instead they should say: "This was Cordelia Maria Sarah's fate, and she had the strength to bear it. Alone." Yes, that, more or less, was how the girl wanted it to be.

Had the mother realized this when, in a letter to a friend, she described how she took leave from her daughter? Yes, the mother saw this part, for she saw what she was able to see and to bear. The fear, the cold sweat of terror, and the lonely, suppressed tears—Mother, why have you forsaken me!—which were with the daughter throughout her life, would haunt the mother only at night, under the onslaught of dreams. In that letter she wrote: "We found her perfectly composed, even cheerful and confident, because first of all it was actually just Theresienstadt and not Poland, and secondly she was accompanying the transport as part of the medical staff; she had two children and an infant to attend to and was already wearing a nurse's outfit and a nurse's cap, which, I believe, filled her with great pride."

23

MAREK AND HALINKA—ESPECIALLY HALINKA. THE first people the girl became aware of and perhaps, where Halinka was concerned, even loved, after she reemerged from the great darkness that had threatened to devour her. Marek and Halinka, who discovered, saw, and confirmed the girl's existence, who gave her the strength and the will to live and to breathe, thawed out her frozen soul and heart and gave her a human face.

Years later, all that remained of the trip to Theresien-stadt in the girl's memory was the suffering in the pale, bearded face of a sick man. He was lying on the floor (was it a cattle car already, or were they still using ordinary trains?), and he and his catheter had been entrusted to the girl's awkward and bewildered care.

The darkness of the arrival is severed by the glaring light of the arc lamps. SS officers shout their commands: All money and all valuables must be handed over immediately, any infraction will be severely punished. The girl is very frightened. When it's her turn in the queue, there in front of the long tables where female inmates inspect the newcomers' luggage and conduct body searches, she obediently hands them her hidden silver cross. To her surprise she is allowed to keep it. Maybe it was only silver-plated; at any rate, the girl has a pure conscience now. Without hesitation she hands over her large handbag. With a practiced hand, the woman at the table cuts open the lining, and to the girl's genuine, horrified astonishment, she pulls out from between the lining and the padding several bundles of hundred-mark bills as well as a few sheets of paper densely covered with writing. The woman calls an SS man, who orders the girl's immediate removal to the prison of Theresienstadt. Probably it is at this moment that the the girl is swallowed up by the darkness.

She is not only sick with fear of the unknown punishment, which will inevitably come, no, the punishment is not entirely undeserved, she knows that. It's true, she had not the slightest idea about the money and the papers in the handbag, but it's also true that she swiped the bag from the attic of the Jewish Hospital. Everyone on the hospital staff went up there occasionally to rummage through the former possessions of deceased or disappeared patients —you could always find something useable. The girl had taken this bag and a pair of high-heeled shoes. The bag, someone had told her, had belonged to a woman who was going to be sent away but made a suicide attempt at the last minute and died in the Jewish Hospital. Of course the girl knew that it was forbidden to take things from the attic. The punishment was—once again—at least partly deserved, she had broken a rule, it was her fault, her mistake.

After many long interrogations by the sad, friendly, old Jewish man who served as examining magistrate in Theresienstadt, the investigators finally believed her. They even found proof of her innocence: the bag had originally been stamped with metal initials. The girl had removed them because they did not match her own name, but the imprint was still visible in the leather. The papers turned out to be lists of furs, household items, and other possessions accumulated in the course of a lifetime, and these lists were signed with the same initials.

The girl was released from prison and assigned to a large barrack that was reserved for children and adolescents without parents. Here she immediately fell seriously ill—probably it was pneumonia—and sank deeper into her darkness. But now she was no longer frightened by it; she used it instead as a kind of cloak of invisibility, a densely woven cover that kept her warm and shielded her from the painful sounds and sights around her.

But the girl was not allowed to remain inside her cocoon. Quite literally, the cloak of invisibility was cut away. It was discovered that she had head lice. Perhaps she had gotten them in prison, perhaps already in the Jewish Hospital in Berlin—in any case, her uncleanness brought bitter shame upon her. Thanks to the efforts of the Jewish camp staff, there were at that time in Theresienstadt hardly any vermin that might have spread death and disease.

The girl's hair was cut off, and for weeks a nurse came to comb her hair with a fine comb to check whether a nit was still hiding on the girl's head. How ashamed she was, sitting by the barrack window on a stool, submitting to that humiliating procedure under the curious and contemptuous eyes of the others! The others were avoiding her, she felt; no one wanted to catch her lice. The mark of leprosy in another form.

But then came Halinka, came and drew the girl out of her darkness into the circle of children and youths who, with their hands on each other's shoulders, were dancing a wildly nostalgic, defiant *horra*—the folk dance their brothers and sisters were dancing out there in the distance under the cloudless sky of freedom. There in faraway Palestine, where "David, King of Israel" danced in their midst and every little Sarah became a queen.

Halinka had already belonged to a Zionist youth movement in Prague and had now in Theresienstadt become the leader of a group of girls in the children's section. She taught them the Hebrew alphabet and songs and dances and spoke confidently of the day when they would have a chance to build "our country." The girl did not understand much of this and remembered even less later on, but the sense of belonging, the feeling of being a member of a group was new, overwhelming and wonderful. Halinka opened a door which the girl had believed would be closed forever.

She remembered the last time she had stood longingly in front of this door, shivering with cold—like Andersen's little match girl—not daring to knock. She must have been ten or eleven years old. She had been brought to the hospital with a severe case

of scarlet fever. Because of the new race laws, it was the Jewish
Hospital in Berlin where she shared a room with a somewhat older
girl who belonged to the Zionist youth movement. Other girls,
friends of the young pioneer, often came to visit and talked with
her through the window. They laughed and made jokes, and occasionally they discussed matters that appeared to be deeply serious,
and for which, every once in a while, they would resort to a secret
language. Those were Hebrew words with which they would
proudly spice their Berlin dialect, but of course the girl did not
know that. She only felt very lonely, rejected, and excluded, someone who wasn't allowed to join in and who didn't belong—much
the way she had felt when she wasn't allowed to join the *Bund
deutscher Mädchen*.

     In Theresienstadt she was allowed to join in. At first
the other girls regarded her with some suspicion, and not just on
account of the lice. For the girl had made no secret of the fact that
actually she was not one of them. Being German and Catholic, it
was only "by mistake" that she had been put among the Jewish girls,
like the princess among the trolls. Nevertheless she wanted to take
part in their activities, but only under her own conditions. Halinka
overlooked these contradictory messages and signals and gave them
no second thought; she saw a lonely, abandoned child and drew
her into the other children's circle. She even granted the girl special
favors: the girl was allowed to "go home" with Halinka a few times.
This "home" was a narrow little shed Halinka and Marek had built
themselves in an attic. An oasis where the desert bloomed, only for
the two of them, but the girl was allowed to visit. She was allowed to
enter the magic circle they had drawn around their love, allowed to
step into a warm light, where Halinka spoke for a long time about
the wonder that had befallen her—Marek. They were both from
Prague, but had only met here, in Theresienstadt. Twenty-two-year-
old Halinka was a little older than Marek and had "a past" that trou-
bled her sometimes—she wished so much that Marek had been "the

first." The girl could well understand this longing for immaculate purity. Halinka consoled herself with a verse she had written for Marek in ornate, decorative letters:

Du bist nicht mein Erster
Du musst schon verzeihn
Aber mein letzter
Der könntest du sein!

To say you're my first one
Would just not be true.
I'm sorry. But my last one
May very well be you!

Did Marek become Halinka's "last one?" Probably. Though not the way she imagined it, not as the man with whom she would have children, with whom she would grow old and whom she would take care of throughout a long life filled with shared memories. Preferably, of course, in Palestine.

A few months after her arrival in Auschwitz, the girl heard that a new transport had just arrived from Theresienstadt. The girl started searching; perhaps she would see a familiar face among the new arrivals. On the cement floor of the empty barrack, the same barrack that was used for internal selections and therefore had no bunks, among the women huddled together in a dense heap, she found the crying and freezing Halinka.

It was actually Marek who was slated for transport, Halinka said, sobbing; thereupon she had volunteered to go, so that she could be with him. Upon their arrival, they were separated, and she didn't know what had happened to her gaunt, delicately built Marek.

That evening, the girl sneaked back to the barrack with a warm sweater and a bowl of soup for Halinka. (Later in her life she would hope that this would be registered to her credit, just like the onion that hard-hearted, stingy Russian peasant woman gave to a starving man, the single onion by whose stem she was later pulled out of hell.)

The next morning the barrack was empty, swept clean, as if no one had ever been there. Marek's and Halinka's traces ended here.

24

MENGELE AND MANDEL, MANDEL AND MENGELE, the blond camp commandant Maria Mandel in Auschwitz-Birkenau and the dark-haired Dr. Mengele, who carried out the selections. The King and Queen of the realm of the dead where the girl had been brought. Why? She never understood it, and hardly ever wondered. Someone had called her, someone had sent her forth to follow this call and obey. Who sent Proserpine forth to serve the lord of the underworld? For that was how the girl experienced it. She was neither executioner nor victim, she had been sent forth to serve, to be used and used up. To become worn and blank like a copper coin that darkly reflects what cannot be said in words.

As if through a gray fog the girl moved among the gray faces of the prisoners, their gray rags, the gray water-gruel and the gray bread. A mute gray silence that would have strangled her with its hard, gray claws if those rulers had not been there in their shining blackness. Mengele's impeccable black uniform and his shining black boots: one kick at the thin blue net of veins at the temple could kill a person. The girl knew it.

Here even the poem, the fairy tale, and the song fell silent (though they would be given back to her later). The girl was filled to the brim with the gray emptiness. Nothing. No one, not man nor thing, not life and not yet death. Not guilt and not faith, hope and love. Love least of all. Words that fell like heavy dead stones into the boundless, bottomless void. Not hate and not anger. Who is there to hate, what is there to be angry at in this empty no-man's-land? Not even pain can gain a foothold in the gray fog of nothingness. Pain can only sink roots in the soil of humanity, it needs to be watered by human tears.

But the girl was still able to recognize and inter-pret the signs and gestures of anger, of pain in others, and—yes, even of love.

When the last trains arrived in Auschwitz-Birkenau, the women of the office were at their post and doing their job. It was their mothers, fathers, and siblings who were arriving now, in the last year of the war. The women of the office were strangled and torn by their rage, which had to be swallowed back and denied. Yes, sir. *"Jawohl, Herr Obersturmbannführer." "Jawohl, Frau Lagerführ-erin."* At the beginning of the war, these women had voluntarily signed up for a "labor transport"; in return, they had been promised that their families would be spared. That promise had now been broken, their sacrifice had been in vain, their survival meaningless. Every betrayal, every cruelty and every iniquity they had commit-ted for the sake of survival and reunion now turned back on them with a mocking grin. When they brutally tore an infant from the arms of a sister, yanked another child from a brother's hand and passed on the children to their grandmother; when they yelled, pummeled, and sometimes herded the young women with blows to the front of the line, all the way to Mengele, was it their hate that impelled them or was it their love? Did they themselves know? Or did they only know that they were close to suffocating on the words they wanted to roar out in a scream as long as the railroad tracks and as high as the chimneys of the crematoriums: "Give the child to Mother! She'll be burned anyway! You, my sister, are young, without a child on your arm or at your hand, you have a chance to survive. To live! Like me! Pay your price and live! Like me."

But that couldn't be said. Only a few hasty words about children and old folks, who would go to another camp, a camp with easier work and better food. It's best for the children . . . for the sake of the children . . . and even in the last year of the war, the newcomers believed this. And then to Mengele: "*Herr Obersturmbannführer*, my sister . . . my cousin . . . childless . . ."

Later, when the young mother was safe behind the camp gate—"*Arbeit macht frei*"—when no one could or wanted to hide the truth from her any longer, she would show no sign of gratitude for the saving of her life, a life for which she no longer had any use. It happened occasionally that one of these women would steal out at night and throw herself against the high-tension barbed wire, in order thus to be reunited with the child she had not been allowed to accompany on this last stretch of the way.

25

THE GIRL SAW AND REGISTERED, SILENTLY, WITHOUT anger, pain, or surprise. It didn't touch her. It didn't enter her consciousness, there was no room there, she was filled with the great, gray void. Sometimes she asked herself vaguely who had sent her out to serve here in the realm of the dead—but basically she knew. It was really so obvious.

After her arrival in Auschwitz, after she had been tattooed with the number that would from now on replace her name—"Prisoner A 3709 reporting for duty"—all her possessions were taken away. For some reason the girl's transport arrived at the camp "unsorted." The selection was carried out later. All hand-baggage, pocketbooks, and other items were deposited in the room of the block leader. The only possessions one was allowed to keep were the clothes on one's body. In the morning, when the prisoners were chased out for their first roll call, all signs of their previous existence had vanished, but on the cleanly swept floor of the barrack, the girl found a piece of paper. Mechanically she bent down, picked it up, and turned it over. It was the picture of her mother, the photograph that had accompanied the girl all the way to this place. Her beautiful mother looking at her with a gaze full of helpless love and pain. Then the girl cried as she had never cried before and would never cry again; not like that.

26

Days and nights passed, and every morning the pile of corpses alongside the barrack grew larger. The women who had died after the evening roll call were layed naked against the wall so they could be included in the morning count. By now the girl knew the meaning of that peculiar, sweetish, stifling smell that hung over the camp. "Like smoked sausage," she had said to someone upon her arrival; now she also knew what the "factory chimneys" were.

On the very first day after their arrival, the newcomers were informed of the facts by the other prisoners, and this with a bitter, desperate, gloating malice toward those who had been spared until now. Surprised, are you? You thought you were being sent to a work camp? That there's what you can look forward to—after the selection. But before the selection came the body search. The women had to undress, everything that was still hidden in one's clothes had to be handed over. The girl tossed her mother's photograph onto the heap. Mandel's deputy savagely whipped the naked women's bodies, just in case it should occur to anyone to hide something, accompanying her blows with the language of the camp, words which themselves cut like whips: *"Los, los, schneller, Mistbienen!"*

The women were herded into a barrack, where, one
after the other, they had to lie down on the table for examination.
The camp doctor, a prisoner, stuck her fingers into the vagina and
the rectum to search for embryos and valuables, both of which
meant death. Mandel herself just stood by, supervising.

Standing in the queue ahead of the girl was an unusually beautiful young woman. During her examination, the doctor
exchanged a few words with Mandel, and when the young woman
climbed down from the table, Mandel affably patted her shoulder:
"So you're still a virgin. Excellent, very nice."

The girl was ashamed, because when her turn came,
they would find out that she was no longer innocent—and yet she
was several years younger and nowhere near as pretty.

THE SELECTION. NOW THE WOMEN KNEW WHAT
would await those who were made to go right and those who had
to go left. Right or left, left or right ... the girl was reminded of
a popular song which Zarah Leander, a Swedish film star highly
esteemed by the Nazis, sang in a film about Mary Stuart: "A white
stone, a black stone, let that be the chain of life." But, the girl
thought, at least the queen wasn't naked as she sat in her tower,
singing and waiting for her sentence and her death.

The women had to line up in a long row and step out
one by one in front of Mengele, who sat casually on the edge of a
table, playfully tapping his whip against a dangling, boot-clad leg.
Or was it perhaps another SS man, the girl could no longer tell.
Just stand straight, look him in the eye, impress him with your
strength and willingness to work. It worked. He nodded his ap-
proval and said: "You're still young, you can still work." The girl
went to the right.

The fate of the other women was literally decided
behind their backs. Mengele, or whoever it was, would scrutinize
them for a moment, they would turn to the right and march off,
toward another SS man who was standing a few meters away, and

behind their backs the sign would be given: thumb up or thumb down. A few tried to sneak over to the other side, a mother wanted to stay with her daughter, a sister with her sister, but all such attempts were discovered and the crying and screaming women were driven with blows to the correct side.

27

THE CAMP STREET STRETCHES EMPTY, DUSTY, AND gray beneath the pitiless, singeing August sun. Coughing and exhausted, the prisoners lie in their bunks. In the office everyone has a plank-bed, but in most of the other blocks there are only niches chopped into a wall. There the women sit hunched over a saved or stolen bread crust, with their wounds, their lice, and the last desperate or dying flame of their will to live. In the penal company's barrack they have plank-beds too, and since it is Sunday, the women aren't marching to work, and no trains will be arriving either. It is calm in Auschwitz-Birkenau, a paralyzing, murderous calm.

The girl feels restless and lonely. She feels threatened by the silence in the camp, it's as if this silence were able to trickle through the tiny, invisible cracks in the great, gray void. Then there would be a hole that could be filled with something, the girl doesn't know with what, but she sees the hole before her, it has the form of a gaping mouth like the one in Edvard Munch's painting, "The Scream." In that hole lurks the scream, the wild, liberating, deadly scream that would shatter the ball of glass she lives in. She can't allow that to happen, because then she'll turn into a "muselman." That is the name for prisoners who decide one day, quite literally, to "give up the ghost." They lie down and wait for death, motionless, with their eyes wide open; he comes quietly and imperceptibly, and no one can tell when a muselman has crossed the border between

life and death, because the breaths and heartbeats are so weak that
they are no longer visible beneath the skeletal ribcage. The last ex-
halation, a slight breath that blows them, light as a feather, into
eternity.

No, she can't let that happen, but who or what
could come to her rescue? Among the women in the office there is
no one who cares about her, they tolerate her, but they scarcely
notice her, they are so much older than the girl, have been here so
much longer, and each of them has her own worries. Nor does the
girl have any images, fairy tales, and poems from whose substance
she might draw strength and consolation. They are all gone, the
insatiable void has devoured everything.

Instead she circles around an image taken from real-
ity, it lures and frightens her, she hardly dares to touch it. Yet it is
as beautiful, as full of unattainable longing as those pictures of
the Mother of God against a sky of gold. Those paintings with their
miniature towns, gardens, and people living their own, protected
life in the background, shining in the golden radiance of mother
and child. Nevertheless this image is dangerous and must—but
cannot—be pushed away and forgotten.

And this is the girl's image:

The beautiful blond woman is standing in front of
Mengele or another SS man with shining black boots. The woman
is holding a child tightly pressed against her body. The eight- to
ten-year-old boy stands before her, and she has wrapped her arms
around him so tightly that the two of them, the woman and the
child, look as if their bodies were joined together.

How the mother ever managed to bring the child
with her into the camp the girl does not know. Maybe the two of
them came with one of those "unsorted" transports from Theresienstadt and she was able—for a while—to hide her child. The SS man
seems to know the woman well, he addresses her by her first name,
he argues and tries to persuade her, begs her to save her own life by

giving over the child, the condemned child. The mother refuses. Finally she and the child are led by a guard through the camp gate down the arrow-straight road that leads to the gas chambers. The woman is holding the child by the hand, she holds herself very erect as she walks, and only bends forward once in a while to say something to the child. There is so much more to say, and the child trots along full of trust, doesn't resist, doesn't seem at all afraid. Maybe the mother is telling him about "the little bird seeking shelter under its mother's wings, and the child resting content in its mother's arms."

THE GIRL SENSES THAT SOMETHING SHARP AND pointed wants to compress the nothingness into a something, determined to give it form and shape. She can't allow this to happen, she must run, run for her life. But where? To Elsa? Elsa in the barrack of the penal company. She is one of the "anti-social" non-Jews who have a black triangle sewn to their striped smocks. Maybe she is a prostitute, maybe something else, but she is from Berlin, and she reminds the girl of the nice housemaids in the squirrel nest, of the smell of cake on a Sunday morning and those exciting, whispered reports about evening adventures after work at a dance-hall called "Resi" where every table has a telephone, which opens up amazing opportunities for unexpected encounters.

The girl pushes open the heavy door of the penal company's barrack and searches for Elsa with her eyes. She hopes that tall, high-bosomed Elsa isn't together with her flat-chested, bony, and vicious friend. The friend doesn't like the girl's sporadic visits to Elsa, and she seems to dislike it even more when Elsa cuddles with the girl while casting a provocative look at her friend. The friend is there, on Elsa's bunk, the girl hesitates a little, but no matter, she has to see Elsa, she won't stay long, just for a little while. The two women see the girl standing in the door, exchange some whispered words and laugh softly. There is something uncanny about this laugh, but the two women, Elsa and her friend, invite

her, smiling, to climb onto the plank-bed. "Well, how's my half por-
tion today?" Elsa asks, hugging the girl tightly. The girl is pleased
by the nickname, only Elsa calls her that, the girl has been noticed,
she is SOMEBODY, not Cordelia, not Dela, but the little half por-
tion, it's a kind of confirmation, no small thing.

The girl looks greedily at the crust of bread Elsa's
gaunt friend is gnawing with her little mouse-teeth. "Are you hungry, kid?" the skinny woman asks stupidly. Of course the girl is hungry, she's always hungry. The two women exchange a conspiratorial
look, and Elsa turns to the girl, whispering: "Maria Mandel often
goes for a walk in the camp on Sunday afternoons." The girl knows
that. "And you've met Mandel, and Mandel was nice to you, right?
Did you know that Mandel sometimes gives out chocolate in the children's block, in the barrack where Mengele keeps Jewish and Polish
children for his experiments on twins?" The girl is aware of that
too, she was present on one of those occasions. "Well, why don't
you take the opportunity and ask Mandel for something to eat when
she walks by?" The girl hesitates, but the thought of a whole loaf of
bread, maybe even a turnip, or even a piece of chocolate, why not,
there are no limits to the imagination—this thought is overwhelming. She promises Elsa and her friend to share what she gets, if
indeed she gets something. Before she has time to change her mind,
the two women push her gently but firmly out of the barrack. She
stands on the empty camp street and sees Mandel approaching her
with her two German shepherds on leashes. The girl casts a glance
back and sees Elsa and her friend peering through the crack of the
door. They have a strange look about them, their faces are rigid and
their eyes glitter with something like hunger and excitement. Suddenly the girl realizes that something is wrong, terribly wrong and
dangerous. But it's too late to turn back, Mandel and her dogs are
already in front of her. The girl stands at attention, and though she
is choked by fear, she manages to rattle off the words: "Prisoner A
3709 reporting for duty, Madam camp commandant, I am hungry."
Mandel looks puzzled, then she laughs and says in a friendly man-

ner: "Well, then go to the supply room and tell them to give you some bread and a can of sardines." The girl scarcely takes the time to thank her, she is already running, not to the supply room but to her plank-bed. She is no longer hungry, and she never looks at Elsa again.

Not much later she learns that on her Sunday strolls through the camp, Mandel will occasionally pick out a prisoner and then let loose her dogs to chase the victim all the way up to the high-tension barbed wire.

28

THE DREAM OF THE GROWN WOMAN.

She returns home, home to the squirrel nest, the house is still undamaged, but uninhabited and long deserted. The woman stands in the hallway and feels the familiar presence of the house around her, she nods in recognition of every corner, every minute detail: behind her is the parents' bedroom, which also served Reinhold as a study on those rare occasions when he was able to flee and retire in peace with his Saint Augustine. Diagonally to the left is the mother's room with its antique secretary and the select set of writing implements made of rococo porcelain and adorned with gold paint, Reinhold's wedding present for his wife. The stairs on the right lead up to the grandmother's room and the rooms of the two little sisters. As a girl she liked to slide down the banister.

Sadly, lost in her thoughts, the woman stands before the small Biedermeier bureau in the hallway, inscribing something in the thick dust with her finger. Everything is there, and everything is past, it was the way it was, and nothing can be changed or extinguished. She is alone with her life, the keeper of all memories, and "After such knowledge, what forgiveness?"

Before her lies the glass-covered veranda leading to
the garden. Here, on summer days, they would have their meals,
which often turned to pandemonium as a result of the mother's
almost obsessive loathing of flies. She was always holding a fly-
swatter at readiness and could at any time smack an unattentive
eater's hand with such suddenness that the soup would splatter
off the spoon and onto the table or even into one's face. She would
make short shrift of the family's protests with a suprised: "But
there was a fly sitting there!" Without a doubt the mother was
imbued with the conviction that the whole creation was the work
of God, but in the case of flies she made an exception. They were
the devil's brood in a direct line of descent.

One Christmas they had put the fir tree here on
the veranda, the woman remembers, and since the veranda with
its rustic furnishings was called the "peasant veranda," the mother
set aside her aesthetic principles for that Christmas feast. Instead
of decorating the tree, as usual, only with silver, gold, or clear
glass balls and candles, this year the decorations had all sorts of
colors, red, green, and blue, and included trumpeting angels, chocolate rings, and lots of silver foil. The woman can smell the scents
of the gas range and the pine needles, she hears Reinhold reading
the Christmas story and sees Uncle Heini disguised as Santa
Claus coming through the snow-covered garden. A white and
merry Christmas.

The door to the garden, shivering out there in the
dank autumn mist, is opened a crack, and suddenly the woman sees
a little black poodle slipping into the veranda. The poodle offers a
distressing sight, its fur is shaggy, its whole little body is skinny,
neglected, pathetic. The woman takes pity on the dog and fetches
a clay bowl with milk, which she puts on the floor of the veranda.
Now the poodle turns around and runs back into the garden, but it
comes right back with a small puppy. The poodle mother carries its
young gently by the skin of its neck, the way cats carry their young.
She runs back out and returns with another puppy. After one or two

more runs she seems to have collected all of her children, three or four of them, and places them around the milk bowl.

The woman quietly watches the poodle family, and in her smile all memories are collected, the present and the past, all tenderness, all sorrow and longing. Her smile is without guile or decption, for it does not deny her bitterness and anger at a world without mercy. At a world in which we are executioners to ourselves as well as to others, and our own and others' salvation as well.

She has come home.

PART II

Ihr führt ins Leben uns hinein,
ihr laßt den Armen schuldig werden,
dann überläßt ihn ihn der Pein—
denn alle Schuld rächt sich auf Erden.
                    —Goethe

It's you who lead us into life,
You let the poor soul err and sin,
and then you leave him to his pain—
For all guilt is avenged on earth.

I

She survived. She became a survivor.

Someone who was left over; someone who had been
pulled across the border between life and death, who had slipped
and stayed behind in the gray mist of no-man's-land. This was "the
land that is not," the land of intangible, unredeemed fear without
language and without words, and therefore without strong, clear
feelings. Love and hate, pain and joy only reached her as indistinct,
muted signals, like voices calling through fog. Half blind, tapping
the ground with the white cane of instinct, she drifted about in the
fog, gliding her fingertips across the braille of life.

She was deaf to human voices, but heard all the
more clearly the signals emitted by the electric barbed wire that
protected and enclosed her realm. The death's-head sign of her
minefield gave warning: This far and no further! Doors that must
not be opened, thresholds that must not be crossed, for behind
them dwells the scream, the scream that must not be allowed to
escape and explode. Deep inside, in the room hung with dark red

silk tapestries, there also lurks the black, sticky slime that wants to ooze out in an all-devouring, all-suffocating flood of impurity.

She is mute. In the beginning was the word, but in the end there were ashes. However, within a short time she had learned to master the sign language of life; to her surprise and contemptuous satisfaction, she discovered that no one wanted and no one demanded anything more of her. On the contrary, anything other and anything more than the agreed-upon signs and gestures—fool's gold or, in this case, horse manure—could, she learned, produce deep consternation.

2

It was her first Christmas in Sweden.

The girl had been invited to the house of a Swedish family renowned and respected for their world-embracing conscience. She was to partake of their gingerbread and their Christmas celebration. And she looked forward to that, naturally. The procession of Lucia, herald and harbinger of Christmas, walking with burning candles through the dark, snow-covered hospital grounds, voices raised in solemn song, had been a grand experience for her. For one moment the girl had believed that the brave breath of the candle flames could conquer the night and melt the block of ice enclosing her little fossil self. "There stands upon our threshold ...," the song said, but the threshold could not, must not be crossed. And yet the unrelieved ache of possibility was an unexpected gift for which she had to be thankful.

The radiant morning of St. Lucia's day reminded her of her trip to Sweden. They had been taken from a labor camp, somewhere near Hamburg, the girl believed, though of course she couldn't be sure. The first to be taken were the sick, a bad sign, and when it was her and the others' turn everyone realized that this was

the end, the camp was to be "evacuated." Someone assured them
that they were going to "Sweden"—to keep them quiet during the
transport, the women presumed. As if that would have been necessary: their senses and feelings were blunted to the point of anesthe-
sia, they were hardly capable of anything but quiet. But Hannah,
the Pole, was still able to crack jokes. As they climbed into the
freight cars and saw that the floor—for the first time—was covered
with straw, she remarked that this last trip was evidently going
to be "first class."

  The girl gave the matter no further thought. She
crouched in a corner and drifted weightless on the billowing tide
of her fever. She was awakened by the train's halting, and she wondered why she wasn't hearing the usual shouted commands and
pounding of rifle butts against the doors. Instead the doors opened
quietly and carefully, and white-clad figures signaled, smiling, for
them to come out. The girl would certainly have obeyed the order,
for of course it had to be an order, but she sensed that her legs could
no longer carry her. Then a few of those white-clad figures came
in with white bowls in their hands and began to feed her, and some
others who hadn't been able to leave the car, white cereal. Everything was white, the gentle, white-clad beings, the bowls, and
even the cereal.

  Then the girl understood that she was dead and that
the story about the white hosts of Heaven was evidently true, even
though she could not detect any wings.

  She realized only too soon, and to her sorrow, that
the "angels" were Danish Red Cross personnel, and that she and the
others were being fed cream of wheat. Thus, despite her overwhelming exhaustion, she was forced to keep struggling, and by the time
they arrived in Sweden, the old reflexes were functioning again.
After the women had showered and been deloused, they had to
step, one by one, before the doctor's table, where they were asked
whether they felt any pain or felt sick in any way. The girl knew
what to do: stand up straight, look him in the eye, show that you're

strong and willing to work! The ploy succeeded—once again. She
was declared healthy—and was allowed to leave. Later, after she
had fainted while standing in line for her meal, she awoke in a
bed with clean linen and saw a middle-aged woman sitting by
her side and felt her stroking her hand consolingly, and sensed
that she would be allowed to lie there in peace, and wished it
could be forever.

After several months of medical care in a hospital for
lung diseases on the outskirts of Stockholm, she was allowed her
first leave, to join the Swedish family on their Christmas celebration. When the girl arrived at the train station where she was supposed to board the little commuter train to Stockholm, she tried as
usual to spell out the signs and guess at their meaning. With a certain pride in her logical faculties, she headed straight toward a sign
saying *"Ingång förbjuden"* (entrance forbidden). Obviously it had
to mean *"Eingang für Juden,"* entrance for Jews. So here was where
she had to enter. She took this completely for granted and was neither outraged nor even so much as startled. When her error was
explained to her, she was only slightly surprised and a little
annoyed at herself for having acted so stupidly.

AT HOME WITH THE H. FAMILY—H AS IN HEART,
throbbing warmly and on the left side for the woes of all humanity
—their house radiantly lit by a thousand burning Christmas candles.
The girl felt hot, she was sweating in the ugly, scratchy rayon dress
she had been given by the Social Welfare department. She was initi-
ated into the rituals of Swedish Christmas, the "dunking in the pot,"
the dried cod, and the Swedish Christmas songs. Some of these,
like "Silent night, Holy night," she recognized, of course, they were
songs she had sung with her family back home in the squirrel nest.
But neither the songs nor the scent of the firs and hyacinths nor the
glow of the candle flames were able to reach her, to shed light into
her darkness and her silence. Like an evil, black bundle, like an ugly
blotch in this luminous Carl Larsson painting, the girl crouched in a

corner, spoiling and destroying the H. family's Christmas spirit. No, she thought, full of hatred, it's not that easy, the card that was dealt out remains on the table, the bones of the dead bleach and rattle in the wind, and what was taken cannot be given back, not even on Christmas Eve.

At first they pretended not to notice. The Swedes are masters of this art, the girl learned after a while, perhaps because there is not much to take notice of. Then the tall, maternally buxom Mrs. H. made a brave attempt to draw the girl in. "But don't you feel comfortable with us, dear?" she begged (?), or threatened (?). "Now it's all behind you, don't you see? Now you have to forget all the horrible things that happened! Soon you will be healthy, and then everything will be different, believe me!"

To put it behind her, to forget, to be healthy—the girl felt despair, rage, and hatred turning into a burning ball of fire in her throat. She still lacked words, but if she had had them, she would have screamed: "But I don't want it behind me, I don't want to get healthy, I don't want to forget! All you ever want to do is 'wipe the slate clean,' as you all so complacently put it. You want to to take my anguish from me, deny it and wipe it away and protect yourselves against my rage, but then you are wiping me out as well, 'eradicating' me, as the Germans put it, then you deny me too, because I am all that. Today, on this Christmas Eve, I am all that!"

But of course none of this was expressed. And many, many years had to pass before it could be expressed and communicated. Not until the girl had become a grown woman and a mother, a helpless, blind, and deluded mother of several children, did she meet a Jewish woman of birdlike frailty and merciless strength who cared for her and was willing to accompany her to the gates of hell and beyond. Together, hand in hand, they descended into the realm of the dead, and the woman became a girl again and looked again into the faces of the damned. She saw them face to face, her mother, Mengele, Maria Mandel, Elsa and Greta, her grandmother during the selection—and herself in various forms.

Her guide was a Jewish woman from Berlin who
loved crazy hats the size of mill wheels and who dared to look the
monster in the face and to say: yes, that's how it was—only worse,
even worse. A hospitable and very lonely woman who pasted paper
angels onto little matchboxes and adorned her barely five-foot-tall
self with long dangling chains. She was a woman who had never
given birth to children, but who became the mother of many to
whom she had given new birth; a woman endowed with the clear-
sighted strength of a Jewish mother, but unsentimental and not at
all prone to foster dependence in others.

For lack of words, the girl cracked a walnut and
hissed: "But I don't want to get well. I wish I were dead! All
the others are dead too. They're still dying. Right now Ilse
may be dying."

A deep silence developed around the girl, and she
knew that she had struck hard—and met her mark. Yet she did not
feel any real satisfaction. She had said both too much and too little.
She felt like a puppy that had soiled the carpet because it did not
know any better, and yet she knew so much more than these people
would ever comprehend. Like the hedgehog, she knew all about
one big thing, but the foxes by the stoop under which she was hiding knew many tricks—and there she stood, ashamed.

After an embarrassing pause the motherly one
regained her composure and said cheerfully, but firmly: "I suppose
it was all a little too much for you, dear, this was your first leave
from the hospital, after all. I think it's best if you go to sleep now."
Maria, the daughter of the house, accompanied the girl on her igno-
minious retreat, holding her by the hand and leading her up the
stairs. She was to spend the night in Maria's room, the room she had
lived in as a young girl, with its white, freshly starched curtains, a
Christmas star on the window and Maria's old teddy bear on the
bed. The girl shyly looked at Maria from the side. Of all the people
here, it was Maria she had least wanted to distress, for it was she

who had invited the girl to the family's Christmas party, and Maria
had always been on her side, and was now too, she could feel it.

They had met in the infirmary at Schonen, where
the girl and her former fellow inmates had received their first
medical care. Blond Maria, the young medical assistant with the
boyish hands—spatulate fingers with chewed nails—which she usually buried in the pockets of her open, white smock, Maria with the
wide hips and the stout legs: she was the first person the girl actually saw, actually noticed after her arrival in Sweden, and the first
person, up to a certain limit, to whom she opened herself up. Maria,
too, had no words, but she saw, and her gray eyes did not avoid what
they witnessed.

Now she sat down on the edge of the bed next to the
girl and said: "Tell me about Ilse."

OH YES, ILSE! THE THOUGHT OF ILSE DYING FILLED
the girl with painful longing. Ilse was the only one of all the women
brought from the camps who had a room of her own—in the main
building of the sanatorium. She lay in the "private station," a name
that was only uttered with awe and envy. All the others were lodged
in the vacant apartments of the hospital staff, which were now called
the "refugee barrack." It was a bit late for refuge, the girl thought.
To find refuge, you'd have to flee, and if they had fled in time, they
wouldn't have had to be survivors. Fleeing, that was something
active, it meant resistance, escape. The women had moved from
one barrack to another, but they weren't refugees, they were survivors. They were left over. By chance. They had been picked up
and collected like spoiled and worthless flotsam after a shipwreck.
Maybe some of it could be repaired, put to use, serve some purpose.
As for her own chances, the girl nurtured little hope.

She had quickly become the lowest in the pecking
order of the ward, and the other women, Polish and Hungarian
Jews, called her a "German swine." The girl knew that she had her-

self to blame for that: being the chosen one came at a price, and she
was still willing to pay it. Without being asked, she had talked about
her parents and sisters back home in the squirrel nest, about her
German-Catholic background, about everything that distinguished
her from the other women. Several times she had received visits
from a Catholic priest, having registered as a Catholic when she
arrived, but now she wished she could ask him to stay away. In the
desolate land the girl lived in, among the bones of the dead, his
words sounded empty and meaningless, even when he spoke with
the tongues of angels.

They didn't fit, those words, they sounded false and
hollow, a placid tolling of holiday bells over a charred land where
there wasn't a blade of grass that had not been singed by darting
flames of fear, where no birds sang and where beneath the shady
trees of the Church's protectory there were no graves. To venture
into this landscape, the inner and outer landscape of the girl, armed
with the so-called "consolations of religion," and with intricate theo-
logical arguments, this—the girl found—was offensive to the point of
indecency. At the very least it was simplicity, but not of the holy kind.

And yet she wanted nothing more than for A 3709
to be Cordelia again, Dela from Berlin-Eichkamp, and to be recognized as that person. Was "German swine" perhaps a step in that
direction? At the same time the girl knew that she was in a hope-
lessly inferior position. Her being the youngest in the whole department was more or less tolerable, but the act of washing herself in
the morning over the basin in the hall was a daily torment. She felt
so misshapen and pathetic when she admired the large breasts and
wide hips of the other women! She herself was flat as a board and
had not had her period yet.

In Ilse's room she could escape all her confusion and
anguish, her shame and disgrace. Ilse knew nothing about the girl's
background, or else she didn't care about it. Red-haired Ilse, her
large gray eyes shining with fever—she was so beautiful, the girl

thought. Her emaciated body was draped in elegant, pastel-colored, fragrant nylon nightshirts, and in her room there was always a lovely smell of perfume and flowers. On Ilse's night table there were always large boxes of sweets, next to the spittoon. She herself ate none of the sweets, but she enjoyed feeding the girl pralines, which she peeled from their colorful tin foil wrappings with her long, slender, carefully manicured fingers.

A fat, middle-aged man visited her regularly. He would sit silently on the edge of her bed and look at her with sad, faithful, dog-like eyes. If he ever said anything, Ilse would reply with a monosyllabic rebuff, and the conversation would die immediately. It appeared to the girl that Ilse felt a weary contempt for her awkward admirer, but that she put up with him because he was the source of all the profusion and luxury surrounding her.

But whenever Jurek stormed into her room on one of his noisy stopovers, Ilse was completely different. Jurek had been a café musician in Poland and was a consummate charmer, glittering and witty—though his wit had barbs. Jurek was capable of being very mean, the girl sensed. In Ilse's room he laughed and joked, ate her candy and occasionally pocketed one or another ten krona note. In exchange he made Ilse laugh so hard that she would get one of her barking, lung-tearing coughing attacks. Then she would wave the girl and Jurek out of the room. She didn't want him to see her in this state, but she especially didn't want to use the spittoon in his presence.

The girl walked with Jurek through the hospital grounds, and also in the woods behind the grounds, where one was actually not allowed to go. She did not like what Jurek did with her there, but she realized that Ilse had chosen her as a substitute. So for Ilse's sake . . . for the sake of the chocolate and the scent of her flowers . . . for the sake of Ilse, who had to die.

Maria sat on the edge of the bed and listened, didn't say much, but listened. That felt good, the girl had been allowed to speak and Maria had understood and wasn't annoyed. Now she wanted to sleep. Maria dimmed the bedside lamp, stroked the girl's cheek, and softly stole out of the room.

MANY YEARS LATER, THE GROWN WOMAN LEARNED Maria's secret. Maria was already dead then, she had taken her own life. A life that had become a secret, shameful, and finally intolerable agony.

Maria was an alcoholic, more precisely a periodic drunk. When she met the girl, she was already drinking heavily, at times to the point of stupor, but was able to hide this from her successful and in every respect well-adapted family. Later that became more difficult. Even though she was able to go on working for a long time, up north in the town where she had moved to hide from her family and her old friends, and even though she was a very popular doctor among her patients, she finally succumbed to the double fear that had become her steady companion. The shapeless, wordless, faceless fear that was her heritage and the sediment of her existence, and fear of that dead end, alcohol, which was the only escape route she knew.

After another withdrawal treatment—she went through several—she took her life.

3

PEOPLE THOUGHT OF HER AS A PERSON WHO was so full of life.

How was that possible, she asked herself later. Was it perhaps because people around her needed those who had survived in the flesh to be alive in spirit as well? So they could believe that nothing was unalterable and that all wounds could be healed? No, that was not the whole truth, the world could also embrace and pity those who were utterly broken, those who were always begging for help, who awakened compassion and mercy in their fellow men. Feelings that announced themselves rather late, but were offered all the more eagerly for that reason.

Or was it just that she had managed to deceive everyone, including herself? She was caught in the labyrinth's hall of mirrors and had lost Ariadne's thread, but she believed that the faster she ran, the sooner she would find her way out. The snake was biting its tail, but the others only saw that she was running, and interpreted this as an unappeasable hunger for life, as an occasionally uncontrolled and heedless sign of a simple joy in living.

Her anger did not permit her to accept the pity and solicitude of others. They would have to try harder than that! She would not allow them to cry over her the way they had sobbed over Anne Frank's diary. This typical adolescent girl's diary, which mercifully ends when the executioners enter the door of Anne's and her family's protected world. Yes, a protected world, despite everything, even if that safety proved to be as treacherous as thin ice. But the journal ends when the ice breaks, and Anne's precocious and oh so forgiving contemplations are strangled by fear and silenced by the blow of a rifle butt against the mouth.

With the touching letters to "Kitty" the world had received its catharsis at much too cheap a price—and pretty young actresses were being given a rewarding part to play on the stage and in the movies. The thought filled her with feelings of hatred.

NORMALLY SHE CAN BE FOUND UNDER "MISSING" in the registry of life's inhabitants, and only when pain and suffering issue their "call-up" does she rise to be counted and say: "Present." Life and reality are there for those who can say: "I generally ... do this and that," "In the summer we always ...," "Every Christmas we ..." Her life is burst and splintered, and when she tries to puzzle out a pattern by putting the pieces together, she cuts herself on their sharp edges.

But there are moments when she is in the world
and the world is in her. Rare hours of shining clarity and fulfill-
ment, when she sets her foot triumphantly on the ground of existence. She loses herself to find herself, she is stirred at the root
of her being, and the survivor comes alive. She is; she exists; and
she wants to write her address in the manner of children:

Cordelia
Stockholm
Sweden
Europe
World
Universe!

This feeling cannot be induced or forced, it comes unbidden, like
an attack, almost frightening her: what if the gods took revenge!

She feels it most often in the little death of eroticism.
Her lovers can never comprehend why she gets so particularly irrita-
ble, restless, and quarrelsome after the most passionate and abandoned embraces. She herself knows and understands how the snake
feels when it sheds its skin, but she cannot and will not reveal her
secret to anyone.

That she exists! In a crowded restaurant, surrounded
by the discreet tinkling of porcelain and silver, by the delicious
aroma of meals and the bouquet of wines, she wants suddenly to
stand up and exclaim out loud, above the muted conversations:
"I am here! I, who was full of lice and scabies and gnawed on raw
potato skins, I, who didn't even have a tin bowl to eat from because
someone stole it from me, I am here! I am eating with a knife and
fork as you are. I order my entrecote medium rare and can send
back the wine if it isn't the right temperature. Life, the goodness
of life, belongs to me, too, and I can enjoy it as you do. Look at
me, I am Job restored to his health and prosperity, I have left

the dung heap outside the city gate and reassumed my rightful place among you!'"

That she exists! Among festively dressed people in a theater or concert hall—she will have no truck with the "What's-so-special-about-that" affectation of the dirty-jeans crowd. It's certainly special to her.

This too is mine! She knows it with triumphant joy. The orchestra is playing for me, the actors receive my applause with bows. Strindberg wrote for me, too, and Mozart, too, he made his music for me, did you know that? No, I myself didn't know it when the mawkish performances of the camp orchestra reached me in the half-light of hunger—*"Heimat, deine Sterne...," "Kleine Möwe, flieg nach Helgoland"*—but now I know it!

She is also abruptly and violently present at one of those painfully beautiful, brittle early summer evenings that enfold all one's unfulfilled longings in a rice-paper-thin, almost transparent cover. Every summer cottage contains a secret of its own, as well as the secrets of bedstraw and lilacs. The rose-blue sky is mirrored in hundreds of highrise windows, and the highrises look as though they might lift off from the stony ground and soar away.

It would have taken no more than a slight, nearly invisible scratch, and the sheath would have burst, the amniotic fluid would have been able to flow unobstructed and take her to other shores—reborn.

Or an early morning on the stoop of the summer cottage. The motherly curve of the blue-and-white breakfast cup in her hands, and the birds' tentative testing of a new day. Yes, it is a new day, the whole creation is new and unsullied, breathing is easy, and even dying would be easy. She realizes and understands that those with a homesteader's claim on life can also "march to paradise with song."

It would be so easy, here on this dawning summer day, to take one more step, trustingly and almost imperceptibly, the step across the invisible, non-existent border. Here, she believes, she would be able to meet with another kind of death, a human death, her own personal death, who comes for her and for no one else, who calls her by her name: Cordelia Maria, it is time, it is finished!

3709, my sister, I want to give back to you the life you were robbed of. This summer morning belongs to you too. Can your death be redeemed in me as well? Someone will close my, your eyes. My grave will be yours, too, one spadeful of earth for me and one for you, one stone for you and one for me.

We both remember the open eyes of the yellow-white skeletons, eyes that no one closed, and we will never forget them. Nor the heaps of bodies growing higher and higher alongside the barrack, nor the hand clutching a crust of bread with a claw-like grip that has to be broken apart finger by finger.

But here, here we too may be granted "a gentle death"; maybe.

4

THE WRATH OF THE SURVIVORS, WHICH TURNS into fear of life.

Year after year the young woman concealed her violent anger. It consumed her, almost suffocated her, but the two of them, the woman and her anger, never got to know each other. She couldn't risk meeting her anger, it was too overwhelming, it would have exploded inside her, it would have become a flashing knife in her hand, to be plunged into her mother's heart. But she did not dare to murder her mother. That would have put an end to Cordelia as well, to the chosen one, who was keeping her vow of fidelity.

The mother wrote a letter to her daughter in Sweden. She wrote that she was working on a new novel, and that one of the characters was a young woman who had been in Auschwitz, a survivor. It was important that every detail of the young woman's memories be accurate. The mother would then recreate these memories in a fictional form. Would the daughter give her an account of the daily routine in Auschwitz? Would she write it down?

The daughter answered, describing her memories as well as she could. Later, when she read the mother's novel, she did not recognize them. It was both too much and too little. There was talk about fire, and no mention of ashes. How could it have been otherwise? It was written by one of the living.

5

HE SAW THAT SHE WAS A SLEEPWALKER BALANCING on a slack rope over the abyss. Unbidden, he took it upon himself to be her safety net.

They met about a year after she had left the hospital against the doctors' recommendation. They met, and she stayed with him. He did not oblige her to stay—it was not in his nature to exercise power of any kind—but he offered himself and his undemanding ways. He never tried to force her into an intimacy she did not have to offer, but he kept an attentive steadfast watch at the threshold of her aloofness. He did not set out to conquer her no-man's-land, but waited patiently for the night to end, for her to awaken. To wake her himself would have been highly dangerous, he understood that.

When she hurt him, it was never a conscious, intentional act, she had no intentions at all, and her consciousness drifted through the shadow landscapes of the underworld. For her, he was a place of rest, of clear replenishment and peace. The most beautiful name he knew was "Ljusvattnet" (lucent water), a lake in Norrland. Yes, she thought, that could be his own name, Lucent Water.

Their son was a quiet, serious child who observed his world with tolerant attention. The mother's aloofness became, in her son, a kind of remote, though not cool, watchfulness. With an open book propped against the edge of the table, the milk bottle in her left hand and the child on her right arm, she would sit for hours, feeding the boy. After a while, mother and child would forget their common undertaking, the mother would become absorbed in her book and the child would stop sucking in his food, which was getting cold; his serious brown eyes observed his surroundings, but he did not participate.

Perhaps, if the father had not been there, the child would have even forgotten to breathe. While the woman lay on her bed in their one-room apartment in one of the worst slum districts of Stockholm, avidly devouring the books the man had lugged to their place from the library, he would be pushing the son in his baby carriage across the rocky hills and among the scrawny pines of the area. The father had something of the child's guileless, defenseless nature, and the son had the moderation of the grown man—they both enjoyed each other greatly. The man became the woman's and the child's lifeline. Like small, light boats moored to the buoy of the mother ship, they drifted, gently swaying, on their separate currents. The man did not try to bring them to harbor, he just saw to it that they were not shipwrecked.

"I guess the safety net should have been more finely meshed," he said with a touch of bitterness many years later, after she had left him. No, she thought, that's not how it was. Love is not enough or can be too much. When she no longer needed his kindness and patience, when she began to take advantage of them, she had to leave. But she always felt grateful for the years of rest by the shore of the "lucent water."

6

WHEN EVERYTHING WAS GOOD BETWEEN THEM, HE would call her "Reisele"; when he felt her slipping away from him, he would angrily call her "Dela."

He lived in the south of Stockholm. On the street side, his apartment had a view of the church of Sophia, that sturdy dame with wide-spread skirts who regally looks down on the formerly poor district of "Vita Bergen." In the early months of summer, the candle-like blossoms of the chestnut trees in the courtyard lit up, and the couple would often stand there in the evening and look into the lighted windows of the apartments in the back. This house belonged to the Jewish community of Stockholm, and the tenants were lower-middle-class Jews. Most of them had come to Sweden before the war, with their earthly possessions stashed away in a few cardboard suitcases held together with string. "The Jews' House," as it was called in the district (without any unfriendly intonation), was an island where a few stranded souls had set up house as best they could with what little they had. Some of them had paid in full for a ticket from a Baltic port to the *"goldene medina,"* America's golden land, but the owner of the ship went bankrupt and the passengers never got farther than Sweden. Others had intended to go to Sweden from the start, but all of them remained alien birds in the Swedish landscape. It was they who had seen to it—very much against the wishes of the native Jews, who were conscious of their Swedish culture—that a Jewish kindergarten and a Jewish school were established in Stockholm. Their Swedish-born, jeans-clad children could now sit on the edge of a cliff on the skerry where the community had their vacation colony, scratch their mosquito bites and say: "Yes, Mama and Papa are coming to see us on visiting day, along with a few Swedes."

Locked in each other's arms the couple stood there, vicariously taking part in the Sabbath rituals of the rear apartments with their festively decked tables, sturdy mahogany tables —the quintessential sign of prosperity and gracious living for Eastern-European Jews—covered with dazzlingly white, starch-stiffened tablecloths and Sabbath candles in brightly polished silver candelabras.

A sort of sympathetic kinship developed between the non-Jewish son of a headmaster, raised in a small Swedish town where there were not likely to be any Jews, and these families wafted up north from their Russian and Polish shtetls. He had never been able to adapt to the neat and orderly ways of the small town, despite the rector's efforts, enforced with a cane, which had left deep wounds and, later, ugly scars. The misfit's separateness turned into the arrogance of loneliness. Living in the contourless, fearful outer regions of reality was the price he willingly paid for the distinction of being one of the elect. Here, in these threatened and precarious border regions, they met and recognized each other. Like Hansel and Gretel, they held each other's hands and strengthened their bond as brother and sister by wandering deeper into the impassable forest, away from the raked garden paths and stale oilcloth smell of the bare kitchen table.

As the older brother, he took the lead and showed the way. He led her to his secret treasures, his books, among which there was a lovingly selected collection of Judaica; he introduced her to his favorite pieces of music, not least among them Yiddish songs—Reisele's song was one of them—to paintings and to Swedish poetry. He gave with great generosity and pleasure, but he set one condition: she must have no other gods beside him. She was to sink her roots and grow in his world, become his creature—Reisele. Cordelia, Dela from Berlin-Eichkamp, was to be extinguished.

If they hadn't had children, it might have worked out.

She herself felt the lure of the will-o'-the-wisps, the promise of freedom from earthly constraints held out to the ailing child by the ghostly Alder King in Goethe's ballad, but she also knew that only survivors have homesteaders' rights in the shadow-land, where one lives with one's back to the world. The living are gripped by sickness and fever there, they freeze and perish, like the child in the poem, even in its parents' arms. No, her children would live. Live!

She began to grope her way out of the forest, into a more pallid, more meager, but also more stable and circumscribed reality. This he could not forgive her, it seemed to him a breach of their bond as brother and sister; he was right, but she had no choice. She wanted her children to partake in a blessedly ordinary day-to-day life, where no witch would lurk inside a gingerbread house, and the good and beautiful queen would never turn into the cruel and ugly stepmother: Even if she herself never found her way to that place, her children would dwell and be at home there, she hoped.

She was deceiving herself, of course: after all, the son and the daughter were her, the survivor's, children. The witch was already in the gingerbread house, the queen was already confined in Hades, and her seductive call was already reaching Proserpine amidst the flowers. Unto the third and fourth generation.

SHE TOOK WITH HER WHAT SHE HAD MADE HER own. The music of the language, the characters of novels, the poems, one or another song or quotation, the chestnut candles, and the black cat, invisible to others, who had lived under the bed they had shared. But the most precious thing he had given her was "Reisele," the part of her he had brought to life with his love. Like an unknown, disregarded heirloom, this part had lain hidden beneath worthless and despised rubbish. He had dug it out and polished it until it took on an unusual sheen, like an old piece of jewelry. Even though, she discovered, old jewelry can be a heavy load.

When she applied formally to leave the Catholic congregation of Eugenia's church, which she still belonged to, in order to join the Jewish congregation, she tried to explain her decision to the old pastor who received her. It wasn't about religion and faith, she said; after all, she had given to the Virgin of the Protective Mantle, for her eternal safekeeping, the patent-leather shoe she had worn for her first communion.

But now something else was at issue: people, the living and the dead, the dead children and the children she had given birth to, and that had been given back to her people through her. Her own life and her children were only partly her own, the greater part she owed to her people, the people she had denied and betrayed. Now, before the cock crowed for the third time, she wanted to try to make amends by avowing her loyalty to the humiliated and insulted. Let the shining black boots march on without her in their campaign to conquer the world, she herself would continue limping on frozen feet wrapped in dirty rags.

But her children, oh, her children, they should sing proudly of "David, King of Israel," and safely of the "buttercups by the grassy slope." They would become Swedish Jews.

The old pastor understood nothing. Annoyed and disgruntled, he stared at her sidelong, wringing his little paws, while his dry old man's voice squawked out all the arguments he had at his disposal. Basically there was only one: Jesus of Nazareth was the Messiah for which her stubborn people had waited and whom they had failed to recognize when he was in their midst. This persistent two-thousand-year wait was nothing more than obduracy and hardness of heart. The grave was empty, he said; He had come, and He would return.

She was tempted to do what the old rabbi had done in the same situation. She would have liked to lead the old pastor to the window, open it wide, and calmly say: "I see no difference." But that would have been foul play. The dice were not cast for the sake of the garment, and the quarrel was not about the crown of thorns. She had nothing against the crucified troublemaker, the emperor's victim; but he of whom the pastor spoke and in whom he professed to believe, was the resurrected and triumphant King of the World. Him she did not know. Nor did she want to know him.

7

AS THE PLANE APPROACHES STOCKHOLM SHE starts crying.

After many years in Israel she is returning as a guest and a stranger to what she once believed was hers to lay claim to. "Everything is mine, and everything will be taken from me." No, it hadn't really been taken away, she had grown out of it or outgrown it, the way a child will outgrow her rag doll or teddy bear. She had left it behind the way one leaves a burnt-out love affair behind, with a grain of bitterness over the flame that no longer sheds any warmth, with regret and nostalgia and, after a considerable time, with deep gratitude.

The landscape beneath her betokens coolness and rest. The verdant fields, the waters and forests have drunk their fill, they guard their solitude and are sufficient to themselves. Isolated red farmhouses and lines of row houses stand scattered like children's toys that will be gathered up in the evening and put back in the toy box. The forests, meadows, and lakes live their separate lives, and will not be disturbed.

No one has ever abused this landscape. This is heathen soil, without history, it has never been gouged with trenches, it knows nothing of bomb craters and fire storms. Never have prophets stood on these mountains cursing these forests, nor did the daughters of Jerusalem tear their clothes here and weep by the shores of dried-up rivers, lamenting a devastated land and their own violated youth. It is a landscape beyond good and evil, it poses no questions and demands no answers.

He who will come to judge the living and the dead will never find the way to this country. How could those who never lived, and how could the survivors be judged?

For a survivor, it was a good land. It was there, offering refreshment and peace, without ever imposing itself, never challenging the survivors to abandon their silence, demanding nothing of them. The bright summer nights and the long, dark winter days, the gentle, steady spring rain and the white, white snow wrapped the survivor in a cocoon of melancholy longing for something that would never happen. Or that had happened a long time ago and now stirred up a vague restlessness like a half forgotten memory. The princess slept a hundred years; meanwhile the hedges around her grew higher and higher. The people wound ribbons around her, and wreaths made of midsummer birch leaves and meadow flowers; the barking of dogs and the sound of hunting horns in the distance are not intended for her.

Many, many years passed before she awoke and realized that this was limbo. The place east of banishment and west of deliverance. No-man's-land and "the land that is not," inhabited by the shades of the good and righteous heathen. They all might have cast the first stone, yet none raised a hand against his neighbor— sometimes, though, against himself.

She, who still had a burnt smell in her hair and in her clothes, began to turn every stone and rummage through every heap of refuse, but all she found were some wood lice or the bones of birds. No skeletons marked by torture, no skulls showing evidence of gold teeth having been broken out of the jaw bones, no emaciated corpses of children.

In the midst of so much innocence she found it hard to breathe, and she realized she had to move on.

PART III

I am that I am.
                    —Exodus 3:14

I

"This is *KOL ISRAEL*–ISRAEL'S VOICE FROM JERUSALEM."

A radio program on the occasion of *Yom hashoa*, Holocaust Day. A woman remembers how she and her family were herded together with all the other Jews on the cobblestone market-place of a small Polish town. Her four-year-old daughter is frightened and cries loudly.

"I tried to calm her down, the SS guards were already looking at us. What if her crying made them angry? I was afraid they would hurt her. Finally I hit her, hard. Then she was quiet."

Later they tore the silenced girl away from her mother.

"But," the surviving mother says, weeping, "when they murdered her, she must have thought it was her punishment for being disobedient. Because I had hit her just shortly before that. I hit her!"

YIZKOR! REMEMBER!

We remember. Every year, when the sirens howl all

over the land, when all traffic stops and the people stand like pillars of salt in the streets, in the schools, and at their places of work. We turn around and remember—the dead and ourselves. The survivors grasp the hands of the dead, and we return to life, to what was and is our life.

In this country we are obsessed with death, someone said once. That is true, she thought, the memorial plaques and monuments for our dead heroes and martyrs are scattered all over the land, and even in the countryside, in the valley of Aijalon, on Mount Gilboa and in the desert of Judea, our insurrections, our victories and defeats are present to us.

But we are also obsessed with being survivors, charred pieces of wood torn out of a fire, eyes that are constantly tearing because of the acrid smoke. We are both hunter and prey; without mercy we chase ourselves out of our lair.

"Hepp, hepp, Jew, run!" We run, therefore we live.

We catch up with ourselves and tear ourselves to pieces, therefore we live.

We feel the earth giving way beneath our feet and take another step toward the abyss, therefore we live.

We give life and our children are strangled with the umbilical cord—unto the third and fourth generation.

2

BURNED CHILD SEEKS THE FIRE.

When she came to the darkened city she knew she had come home. This was a reality she could recognize, here she would stay. She had come as an observer and reporter, but her knowledge of the past and her visions made her a participant.

It was during the first days of the Yom Kippur War. The whole country was holding its breath, cowering in the dark, in extreme concentration and tension, like a threatened animal before it leaps out to kill its attacker. The threat of destruction and the people of the land looked each other in the eye with the familiarity of recognition. The survivors returned to the only form of life, the only task and challenge they had learned to master—the struggle for survival. But, she felt, here human beings and the forces of destruction were meeting as combatants, the outcome was not predetermined, not this time. This was fair play. If destruction won, it would not be because the victims, paralyzed and petrified by the sight of the Beast, contributed to their own ruin. This time the threat had a human face, the face of the enemy. He had to be fought, could perhaps be defeated, but he also could be recognized and respected. That is why, and it is the only reason why, in resistance and respect, the survivors regained respect for themselves. They would not voluntarily dig their own graves, but neither would the dead of the enemy be left to the foxes and dogs of the desert.

IN A FIELD HOSPITAL IN THE SINAI DESERT SHE MET her son, all her sons. She stood amidst the noise in the hot desert sun as the army helicopters returned from the other side of the Suez Canal and landed with their bloody harvest. Stretchers were unloaded, one after another. The soldiers ran to the operation tents carrying the stretchers and bags filled with blood-plasma, ducking as they ran under the propeller wings, which were still whirling.

At that moment she saw him. The blond boy was lying prone on one of the stretchers, his face was turned toward her, she looked into his eyes, which were vacant behind a film of pain, saw the dried blood on the left side of the uniform shirt and saw that this was Daniel, her son, who had died of cancer at the age of ten. Her Daniel or the Daniel of another mother, that didn't matter, she was a part of her people, a member in the covenant of the indelible seal. An Isaac bound to the sacrificial altar, a Yankele with a bright yellow *Judenstern* on his outsized coat, his thin face shaded by a cap, holding up his arms, and a Daniel who had been hit in the side by a shell fragment, all our sons at all times. The cycle of our death and of our resurrection in different form and guise, and still we can say:

"I am!"

Jerusalem, November 1983